Churches with an Evangelistic Life-style

ON THE GROW!

Churches with an Evangelistic Life-style

ON THE GROW!

by
Charles R. Shumate
illustrated by Richard Stump

Published by
Warner Press, Inc.
Arlo F. Newell, Editor in Chief
and
Board of Church Extension
and Home Missions
Anderson, Indiana

All Scripture quotations, unless otherwise indicated are taken from the King James Version ©1972 by Thomas Nelson or The Holy Bible, New International Version ©1978 by New York International Bible Society.

Copyright ©1984 by Board of Church Extension and Home Missions.
All rights reserved.
ISBN: 0-87162-294-7
Printed in the United States of America

Contents

v

Foreword

Evangelism is a busy word in the Christian world today. Theologies of evangelism, conferences on evangelism, methods of evangelism abound. All of them are necessary and helpful, but conferences and theologies and methodologies must all be translated into the real world of hurting, lonely, lost men and women.

That is why the local church must always be a nerve center for authentic evangelism. For it is out of the church that waves of evangelism should flow and it is into the church that the results of evangelism should come.

Charles Shumate has done us a good service in this regard in his new book ON THE GROW. Out of his deep and warm experience as an evangelism leader in the Church of God in Anderson, Indiana, he has given us a study which I warmly commend to evangelistically concerned pastors and lay people of all denominations.

I commend this book for six reasons. First it is *biblical*. The inspired Word of God must always be our infallible rule of faith *and practice*. Charles takes us to the source and the biblical models in Jesus, in Paul, in the other apostles. Theirs is the standard by which all evangelism must be judged.

Second, it is *situational*. The Word of God is always true in every situation, but it never comes to us in a vacuum. God chose a particular time and place for his Son, our Redeemer, to be incarnate in the world. And the saving grace of his Son still comes into the concrete situations of men and women. I find it fascinating that this book clearly relates the communication of the gospel to a wide variety of actual situations, detailing the economic and social contexts in which people are to be reached.

Third, it is *congregational*. The uniqueness of this book is that we actually see into a variety of congregations, of different types and sizes, communities of people who are very human, but who are also touched by God's Spirit. Here is not theory to be discussed, but practice to be taken seriously.

Fourth, it is *pastoral*. I like the way in which Charles allows a number of pastors to open up their hearts and speak out of their experiences. These are men who know what it is to weep and laugh and hurt and counsel and pray and evangelize with very real people. Pastors and lay persons alike will be able to sense the shepherd's heart.

Fifth, it is *practical*. For all the above reasons

and others, evangelism leaders in the local church will be able to take out an idea here, a workable plan there which they can test and try.

Finally, it is *motivational*. Evangelism is not first a program or a plan. It is first a passion. It is a throb in the heart of God, a sob in the spirit of the evangelist. The fire must be stirred up for evangelism to happen. Charles Shumate's book will help many of us to say again with Paul, "Woe is me if I preach not the gospel."

Leighton Ford, Evangelist
Charlotte, North Carolina
Billy Graham Evangelistic Association
Chairperson, Lausanne Committee for
   World Evangelization

J esus Christ sent forth his disciples to be his witnesses. It was not an assignment that someday they would fulfill, as they matured in knowledge. It was a fact of their present experience of grace and whether or not all its implications were perceived, their manner of life was a testimony of the power of God to change the world.

Witnessing by its nature is the visible manifestation of the living Savior in the lives of his people. It is not something worked up, but lived out—the reflection of him who indwells us by his Spirit. The witness may be obscured, even distorted through our lack of conformity to Christ, but it can never be avoided.

The necessity for personal holiness is clear. For only in the measure that our lives are set apart for God can we become a vessel meet for the Master's use. Though our comprehension of his will may be small, still we can offer all that we know of ourselves to all that we know of him, even as we continue to grow in his likeness.

Whatever our calling and gift, there is a place in his ministry for us all. He appoints the sphere of service; our part is to obey—to live intensely transparent before him and his people.

Beyond prayer, our priesthood finds its most relevant expression in relationships that are established with persons around us. Here we can minister every day. As we seek to meet evident needs, an environment is created whereby the gospel can be communicated with conviction to receptive hearts. In God's own time, when the soul is properly cultivated and the seed planted, there will come a harvest.

Faithfully the Church is gathered by the Spirit, forming a corporate fellowship of saints, the body of Christ. Local congregations assemble to study the Scripture, receive the sacraments, and build up one another in love. To facilitate the body life, some persons are specially called to provide leadership, particularly in equipping the body for the work of ministry.

A properly functioning church invariably will grow, both in spiritual depth and in numerical breadth. Vital holiness cannot be self-contained; the Spirit of God insists upon making Christ known, and as he is lifted up, people are constrained to call upon the name of the Lord and be saved. Little wonder that the disciples at Pentecost had such boldness to declare their faith. When hearts are full they easily overflow.

Evangelistic outreach to the world is not our only ministry, of course. But it is the most crucial. For without it, there would soon be no church. We must, then, make disciples who will let the Spirit use them to reach others, teaching disciples in turn to do the same, until finally the gospel of the Kingdom reaches the ends of the earth. If we would take this commission to heart and live by it, through the process of reproduction, the world could be reached for Christ in our generation.

While implementing this vision in the local church will not come without dedication, there must also be resourcefulness. Ways must be found to mobilize the saints for action. Often in this practical area we flounder for lack of direction.

That is why this book will prove so helpful to persons who believe in dynamic church growth. It describes in forthright conversations with pastors how their congregations have responded to the challenge. No claim is made that the churches are perfect, but they have developed programs that God has used in their communities to bring people to Christ. That something was effective in one situation does not mean that it will be equally successful in another, but an approach may be suggested that, with adaptations, might work elsewhere. The great variety of the selections adds to the appeal.

The author has done his homework well. As the Director of Evangelism in the Church of God, he has traveled widely, and knows what is happening across the American scene. What is most refreshing, he does not write as a mere theoretician, but as a practicing evangelist and former pastor.

In the unfolding of the story, almost anyone can find a place to identify. It gets down to basics, and prods us to consider more realistically the life-style of the gospel. I can only hope that its message will not go unheeded.

Robert E. Coleman, Director
School of World Mission and Evangelism
Deerfield, IL

Acknowledgments

May I acknowledge my indebtedness to those who have played a role in the development of this book, either directly or indirectly. I wish to thank my staff colleagues at the Board of Church Extension and Home Missions. I also wish to thank my wife, Laretta, and our two cherished daughters, Chausette and Chara, who have patiently waited while I have traveled and researched these pages.

The local churches described in this volume deserve the major credit for making this book possible. I am grateful to each pastor you will meet in the following pages for granting an interview and sharing the stories of their evangelistic congregations. I appreciate each pastor's openness, warmth, and kindness during my on-the-scene visits and personal interviews.

I am especially indebted to my staff colleagues David A. Telfer, Marvin J. Hartman, and Louis P. Meyer for their encouragement and guidance in the project. I appreciate the personal enthusiasm and editorial guidance given by Arlo F.

Newell, editor in chief of Warner Press. Special thanks as well to Joseph D. Allison, who helped to smooth out awkward phrases and who field-tested this book as a midweek study in the congregation he pastors.

Without the capable assistance of Norma J. Brandon, Sherry Sitzler, Ruth Carroll, Ruth Ann Hausman, and my wife Laretta, the tapes and manuscript would not have been prepared for publication. I thank God for each of these courtesies.

Charles R. Shumate
Anderson, Indiana
July 6, 1983

Introduction:
Evangelism as a Style of Life

Our jetliner was cruising above the craggy hills of New Mexico. Brilliant sunshine glimmered on the wingtips as we sailed through the clear blue sky. But I paid no attention to the scenery below; I was too engrossed in the conversation one row ahead of me.

In one seat was a trim, middle-aged man with a troubled expression on his face. He was saying, "I hate to fly. Airplanes give me the jitters—always have. I just took this new job in sales and I have to travel a lot. Guess I've gotta get used to it. But every time I hear a squeak or a whine, I think we're about to crash."

"I know how you feel," said the man beside him. I noticed he wore a blue pilot's uniform. Off-duty, I assumed.

"I was scared of flying for a long time," the man in the uniform continued. "I didn't know whether I could trust a plane to keep me airborne. Always thought it would stall and crash.

But the more I learned about flying, the more I trusted the plane and the pilot." He went on to explain the basic principles of flight—how the wings create lift, how the rudder stabilizes the plane, how radio instruments keep the pilot on course, and so on. This fascinated me. As he talked, I felt less afraid of flying myself!

Finally, he said, "There came a day when I learned I could trust my life to another Pilot. His name is Jesus. I'd like to tell you. . . ."

Just then, a chime sounded. "FASTEN SEATBELTS" appeared on the lighted sign overhead.

"Hear that hum?" the uniformed man asked. "That's the landing gear. A hydraulic pump is moving it into place. We'll touch the runway at Albuquerque any minute now." We felt a slight bump. "There! Another perfect landing! Tell you what—I'm going to stop at the airport coffee shop. Care to join me?" His seat mate grinned and nodded.

I wish I could have heard the rest of their conversation. But I'd heard enough to know this man had made evangelism his way of life. He knew even a casual conversation might give him an opening for the gospel—and he was ready to present the gospel in a natural, friendly way. He had an evangelistic life-style.

Evangelism was born of good news: good news about God's purpose, power, and love (Rom. 1:16) and good news about Jesus and our relationship to him (John 3:16). That good news is concerned with the total person and all of life. The Christian is sent into society to tell and live this gospel.

The early church proclaimed the Good News with no fear of negative response or indifference (Acts 17:30-31). The message was given regardless of the result. Evangelists as we know them are mentioned only three times in the New Testament (Eph. 4:11; Acts 21:8; 2 Tim. 4:5). This does not imply that evangelism was a limited activity in the early church; rather it highlights the fact that evangelism involved the entire church. All Christians were expected to witness. Historically, as professional ministers emerged, lay people were less inclined to witness for the Lord. That was considered the pastor's work. At least Christians thought their pastors were better qualified. Yet the New Testament pattern of evangelism involved the total fellowship.

That vibrant New Testament pattern calls us to redefine our modern understanding of evangelism. Genuine Christian evangelism is *life-style evangelism*. Life-style evangelism is not something you go and do; rather it is something you do as you go. It is not done just in visitation for the church on Monday night, but it takes place in the normal flow of our daily communication and interaction with people. We can further sharpen our focus on evangelism by calling it "that life-giving, life-sharing expression of one's faith that begins with the new birth and ends with the last breath. In its simplest terms, it is evangelism as a style of life."[1] This, then, is life-style evangelism:

The commitment of one's life;

The integration of life and witness;

The spontaneous expression of Christian faith.

A life-style view of evangelism allows God's people to be natural and creative as they bear witness to Christ, like that man on the plane to Albuquerque.

Authority to Evangelize

Our authority to bear witness to Christ and to bear witness as a way of life, is inherent in the good news about Jesus Christ. Jesus is the Word of God made flesh (John 1:14). All things were created by him and for him (Col. 1:16, 20). He is the foundation of life (1 Cor. 3:10-11). If these statements about Jesus are true—and they are—then no other authority to evangelize is required.

An American magazine editor was making a tour of Java when he met a traveling Hindu holy man. As they had tea together, the Hindu said he hoped to visit America as a missionary— not so that he could convert people to Hinduism, but so that he could show them that all the great religions teach basically the same things. He took a napkin and listed a few of them. Love your neighbor. Live at peace with all men. Treat others as you'd want them to treat you, and so on.

"All the great religions teach these things," the wizened little Hindu said. "So why don't we use religion to bring all men together? Why not tie the heart cords of all humanity with the teachings of Mohammed and Gandhi and Jesus?"

The editor liked this idea. So when he got home, he wrote a glowing editorial that called for a World Parliament of Religions. "Let the great religions cease explaining their differences to each other," he wrote, "and begin to chart the elements of basic unity that could serve as the building blocks of common action."[2]

Noble words, aren't they? And many people would like to think they could melt all the world's religions together like that. But Christianity won't fit in the pot. The Lord of the Christian faith is the only begotten Son of God, the only Savior of the world. The Bible says so. If we pretend that Jesus were merely another great teacher of truth, we deny the Bible and deny Jesus himself. He stands alone. And he says, "When I am lifted up from the earth, I will draw everyone to me" (John 12:32, TEV).

This is why we draw other people to Christ. They have no other hope; we have no other authority.

Motivation for Evangelism

Echoed in the Great Commission of Matthew 28:18-28 is Jesus' earlier command to "go out into the highways and hedges, and compel people to come in" (Luke 14:23). So our initial motivation to act springs from our own relationship with Jesus Christ. We hear his command to go.

When we have experienced new life in Christ, we have a message we can share with others (Matt. 12:34). "The good news is a message centered not in the immovable type of a printed page, but in the moving testimony of a personal proclamation."³ A Christian witnesses out of his or her personal experience of love's forgiveness and acceptance. The reality of Christ motivates him or her to tell others about Christ.

In addition, we are motivated to evangelize when we realize the tremendous needs around us. People today are looking for some definite expression of the gospel. They want good news. Christianity provides this in Jesus' declaration that he is the way, the truth, and the life (John 14:6). Jesus Christ alone reveals God to the world. Jesus Christ alone can save the world. This conviction evokes our deep, inner passion and fiery enthusiasm for evangelistic outreach. So life-style evangelism is not only our duty, but also our marvelous privilege. From our relationship with God and our own experience of salvation grow a love for people and a desire to share the love of Christ with them.

The well-known Baptist pastor Jack Hyles was mowing the lawn one day at his parsonage in Texas when his wife asked him to go to a neighbor's house and borrow a cup of sugar. He took the empty cup and since the neighbor was one of his church members and a good friend, he marched right into the house and said, "Hello. Is anybody home?"

There were thirteen people in the living room—visitors, all dressed in their finest clothes. He had on faded blue jeans and a holey T-shirt.

The lady of the house swallowed hard and said, "This is my pastor."

After a moment of awkward silence, Dr.

Hyles decided he might as well take charge. So he started introducing himself to each person in the room, saying, "How do you do? I'm Jack Hyles. Are you a Christian?"

The last young man said, "No—but I've been thinking about it."

"Well, I can help you think about it right here," Hyles said.

They got a Bible and Jack Hyles won him to Christ.[4]

Jesus set the early Christians aflame for evangelism. They understood that Jesus had come to seek and save the lost; they knew that was the supreme purpose of his incarnation and atonement. Michael Green says, "Evangelism was the very life blood of the early Christians: and so we find that 'day by day the Lord added to their number those whom he was saving.' It could happen again if the church were prepared to pay the price."[5]

Models for an Evangelistic Life-style

The Bible shows us the early church as a model of an evangelistic life-style. The Church of God also finds two other biblical models for evangelism: the life of Jesus and the ministry of the Apostle Paul.

Jesus

Jesus' life proved that God was "in Christ . . reconciling the world to himself" (2 Cor. 5:19). God reached the world through Jesus, and Jesus reached the world through life-style evangelism. As early as his first visit to the Temple while he was yet a young boy, Jesus expressed his urgent

7

desire to do his Father's work. He later told his disciples, "the Son of man also came not to be served but to serve, and to give his life as a ransom for many" (Mark 10:45). And again, in the simplest terms of evangelism, Jesus spelled out his purpose: "For the Son of man is come to seek and to save the lost" (Luke 19:10).

During his earthly ministry, Jesus served a broken humanity. He heard the cry of the sick. He felt the guilt of a sinner, the pain of the hungry, and the loneliness of the prisoner (Matt. 25:31-46). In response to those needs, Jesus preached the gospel to the poor, healed those sick in mind, body, and spirit, and liberated those in virtually all forms of captivity (Luke 4:18). Jesus drew from the servant passages of Isaiah (42:1-4; 49:1-6; 50:4-11; 52:13—53:12) to understand his mission of service. He rejected the world's standard of greatness, proclaiming instead that greatness lies in the role of servant (Mark 10:42-45). Indeed, as Jesus pointed out, the greatest title one may receive is not master or father or teacher; it is servant (Matt. 23:6-11). In his life-style and even in death, Jesus exemplified servanthood.

In discussing the life-style evangelism of Jesus as recorded in the New Testament, Louis Sperry Chafer says, "Of the forty-three evangelistic references, about twenty-five refer to personal work with individuals by Jesus; twelve refer to public work of Jesus without the individual being personally interviewed; about five refer to neither public nor personal evangelism. . . . Of the twenty-five instances of private methods, most record conversion; of the twelve instances of public mass approach, most record no conversions."[6] In other words, though Jesus preached to great crowds, mass meetings were not the strength of his evangelism. The real impact of his message came in one-to-one confrontation. The Master mixed with all types of people, regardless of background, race, age, sex, or position. He could speak to a Roman concerned about his servant (Matt. 8:1-13), a woman with an afflicted daughter (Mark 7:24-30), a delegation of inquiring Greeks (John 12:20-21), or the outcasts of society (Luke 19:10), and never lose his compassionate, one-to-one concern.

This life-style evangelism is vividly portrayed in the healing of the blind man (John 9:1ff). After the man had been cast out by the Pharisees, Jesus sought him out to confirm that the man had placed his full faith in him (John 9:35). Jesus ministered to all the man's needs, physical and spiritual. Through one-to-one life-style evangelism, Jesus touched the real needs of the people he served.

Although Jesus met the needs of people wherever he found them, he spent most of his time with a special group, his twelve disciples. He taught the disciples to be evangelists. Almost everything the Lord did with them or said to them aided this process of training and discipling. By his example and by specific instruction, he prepared the disciples to carry out his commission. After very careful teaching, Jesus sent them out on missions of preaching and healing (Matt. 10). Later he sent out seventy disciples with essentially the same commission: to find people with moral, physical, and spiritual needs and share the good news of the Kingdom (Luke 10:1-16). In his own one-to-one ministry and in the training of his disciples for the Great Commission, Jesus taught life-style evangelism.

Paul

Although Paul was not one of the twelve disciples, his great life mission embodied life-style evangelism. The Book of Acts pulses with his work as a life-style evangelist. In Acts 20:20 he summarized his ministry in Asia by saying he had witnessed to them "in public and from house to house." With believers and unbelievers alike he emphasized his one-to-one witness. Paul depended on public witness to arouse interest, and when the crowds dispersed, he became a personal witness to those who remained behind (Acts 17:4, 33).

In his personal witness, Paul willingly admitted his shortcomings; yet he knew Christ lived in his weaknesses as well as his strengths. He opened himself to those he met, varying his approach according to their need. By the river at Philippi, for example, Paul spoke the Word to a group of women gathered for prayer; as a result, Lydia was converted (Acts 16:12-15). In his sermon on Mars Hill, he argued logically with hard-shelled Greek philosophers and even won some of them to the Lord (Acts 17:22-34).

Whatever the approach, Paul so confronted unbelievers with the claims of Christ that churches sprang up wherever he went. Paul took others with him as he traveled, as Jesus had done, training them to spread the Word to yet more people and more places. Barnabas, John Mark, Silas, Luke, Gaius, and others benefited from training under Paul.

In his letter to the church at Ephesus, Paul says Christ conferred the gift of evangelism on his followers. In his second letter to Timothy, he urges the younger man to "do the work of an evangelist" (2 Tim. 4:5). This encouragement and training, a dominant part of Paul's ministry, insured that life-style evangelism would continue when his own work had ended.

The Early Church

The early church grew through an evangelistic life-style. The church traces its beginnings to the coming of the Holy Spirit on the Day of Pentecost. Almost immediately after his coming, Peter and John went to the Temple to pray. There they met a lame beggar, and called upon the name of Christ to heal the man. Having met that need, they called on the authority of Christ to preach to the gathering crowds. So strong and clear did Christ sound the evangelical note through them that five thousand men believed.

Soon after this, Jewish leaders barred believers from their synagogues. For the first three hundred years, Christians owned no church buildings; and since persecution became more severe, they were forced to meet in private homes. The New Testament often refers to "the church in thy house." Since the private home was the center of Christian work, life-style evangelism was easy and natural for believers.

Believers came from all walks of life. Each one's distinctive personality and abilities became tools for God's work. According to Acts, the early Christians witnessed in the Jerusalem temple (5:12), on street corners (2:14-36), in the marketplaces (17:17), at city gates (14:17), and in jail cells (16:31). C. E. Autrey observes:

> The church at Jerusalem was an evangelistic church. It grew rapidly. What were the reasons for the great growth? The answer is found in Luke's statement, "And the Lord added to the church daily such as should be saved." First it grew daily. Every day new converts were made and added to the church. Its growth was not spasmodic but by continual daily advance. In the second place it grew through the help of God. Its growth did not come merely through human ingenuity. "The Lord added . . . those who had been saved." The church members, imbued with the spirit of God, gave their witness, and the Holy Spirit used their testimony. Growth came through a daily witness empowered by the Lord.[7]

An Evangelistic Life-Style Today

How shall we model today's church on the examples of Jesus, Paul, and the early Christians? We can do it only by returning to life-style evangelism. The modern church must recapture the enthusiasm that caused the New Testament church to burst forth with the ripened seeds of the gospel, scattering them to every garden plot and pathway of their daily lives. Evangelism must become again the natural result of being saved—not merely a method or technique used by a few specialists. We must realize that evangelism is the life work of *every* believer.

Our enthusiasm to witness for Christ grows as we further understand what God is doing in the world. The Bible tells us what he's doing. From Genesis to Revelation, one paramount fact shines forth from the Scriptures: *God is a loving and caring God.* Both the Old and New Testaments reflect that assurance of 1 Peter 5:7, "He cares for you." Since God cares, his people care. The more they study, the more they respond with loving and helping other people in the name of Jesus.

Every Christian must have personal prayer and communion with God. These quiet times with him are crucial to maintaining our enthusiasm for the work of evangelism. As we pray, our concern for others becomes more consistent. Any pattern of evangelism is rooted in humble, earnest prayer.

The driving force behind life-style evangelism is the Holy Spirit flowing through us. The Holy Spirit makes us realize that God is the true evangelist; we are but his instruments. The source of our evangelistic power is the Holy Spirit (Luke 24:49). Leslie Woodson wrote, "Evangelism is simply sharing the Lord through the power of the Holy Spirit."[8] The Spirit leads us to offer Jesus Christ as life's only dependable

13

center and guide.

As the Church grows more mature through serious study, prayer, and the leading of the Holy Spirit, believers will see their evangelistic mission with greater clarity. As God's people through his "new convenant in Christ Jesus" (2 Cor. 3:6), Christians continue the lifework of caring for and blessing all nations, a responsibility once entrusted to Israel (Gen. 22:18). In doing so, the Church continues the ministry life-style of Jesus. T. W. Manson, in his work *The Church's Ministry,* concludes, "There is only one essential ministry in the church—the perpetual ministry of the risen and ever present Lord, himself."[9] Jesus ministered in Judea, Samaria, and Galilee, and now he continues his ministry around the world through his body, the Church. Andrew Murray said, "Christ's mission is *the only reason for our being on earth;* were it not for that, He would take us away."[10]

Paul says in Ephesians 1:17-22, "God . . . the Father of glory . . . gave him [Jesus Christ] to be the head over all things to the church, which is his body." Jesus' identification with his people is also clearly heard in Jesus' words to Saul the persecutor on the Damascus Road, "Saul, Saul, why do you persecute me?" (Acts 22:7). The living Christ suffers, preaches, and ministers in all Christian people. Only as Jesus ministers in and through us are we the Church; and only as he ministers in and through us is our ministry a Christian ministry. While the Church helps its own members (Acts 2:44-45; 6:1ff), its ultimate mission is to share God's love with the community outside. As I said before, Jesus' life-style radiated love and care for a broken, hurting world (Matt. 11:28-30). Jesus' parables of the good Samaritan (Luke 10:25-37), the lost sheep (Luke 15:3-7), the lost coin (Luke 15:8-10), and the lost son (Luke 15:11-32) forcefully portray his care and concern for persons. Of course, the supreme evidence of his care was his death on the cross (John 3:16; Rom. 5:8).

Jesus' life and death call his followers to care for all people, even their enemies (Matt. 5:43-44). What Jesus said of his own life and ministry applied with equal force to his church: "The Son of man came not to be ministered unto, but to minister" (Mark 10:45). Jesus commanded us to continue his ministry of love and care. Within that call he provided for varied ministries; however, no provision is made for a nonministering church or nonministering members. There were no drones or nonworking Christians in the New Testament church. To be in the body of Christ is to be a part of his working body. The New Testament church and the genuine Church of today must care about people in the community who do not know Jesus Christ.

The Local Congregation

Critics like to ridicule the local church. Some said during the 1960s and 1970s that the church was dying. Yet the local church is God's basic tool for world conquest. The church has a duty to prepare its members through study, worship, and training so that they will be effective witnesses during the work-a-day week. Instead of making the worship service the climax of the week, the church must use the worship experience as a period of preparation for the real climax—serving as the men and women of God during the week. Possibly the ministry of the church members during the week can be only as effective as their worship is *affective*. When worship changes our lives, we're ready to change the world.

Wherever laypersons are involved in the world, the church touches the world. "Lay people, and they alone, in their daily lives and occupations encounter the society in which they live. They form in a very particular way the spearhead of the church's true mission."[11] Lay people represent the church and should consciously present a witness for Jesus Christ in relevant ways. Only as God's men and women are scattered into the world as his witnesses can God change the course of current events.

The church must involve every member in her mission. Lewis Drummond emphatically writes, "Unless the church recaptures and implements the principles of a lay-centered ministry, I see little hope of fulfilling the Commission to evangelize our day."[12] Jesus calls us to stop putting the concerns of the church first and to undertake the radical task of healing the wound of the entire inhabited world. That kind of effort will require "a priest at every elbow." The all-out effort of every Christian is essential.[13]

This is what we mean by the "priesthood of

all believers." It's more than just a catchy slogan to entice members to take jobs in the local church. Every Christian is called to be a priest of God. All believers should witness to Christ in every arena and station of life. The words of Martin Luther strike us hard: "Christians are to be little Christs." That's an awesome responsibility. But if God's Word is to change the world in which we live, the Word of God must become flesh again—in the lives of his people in the midst of everyday life.

The Journey to an Evangelistic Life-Style

A congregation never just happens to have an evangelistic life-style. It comes about only when God's people pray, prepare, plan, and work for it. Evangelism is not optional for the Church; it is absolutely imperative. The Church must live the good news and then share it. When the Church dies to self and lives for Christ, the journey toward an evangelistic life-style begins.

The local church has to establish its purpose and priorities. Each church must ask itself why God brought this particular body of believers together at this point in history. What is the Church going to do with the message God has given it?

James E. Williams recalls how he used to frequent the train station in Alexandria, Indiana, when he was a boy, to watch the steam locomotives come and go. He said that the most exciting event to his boyish mind took place when the conductor gave the signal for the train to leave the station and the engineer opened the throttle. The boiler had a full head of steam, and all of that steam was translated to the driving rods. The wheels spun. Sparks flew. A great screech was heard. But the train did not move.

"I'm afraid that's often a picture of what we do in the church," he said. "We throw all of our energy into a dizzying round of activities. There's much noise, much motion, much evidence that something great is going on. But the church does not move forward because souls are not being won."

Of course, let's be sure we're building an evangelistic life-style with the right motives. If we win others to feel good or to gain approval of others, we produce nothing for the Kingdom. The right motive for evangelism is our gratitude for God's gracious love, shown when he gave us his Son. When we are truly grateful for God's love, we naturally will want to tell others. We will make evangelism our way of life. When the walls of a person's life tumble down, and that liberated believer feels secure in Jesus, he or she reaches out in love to someone else.

The congregation communicates this love to people who come to church looking for something different from what they find outside. The very atmosphere of the worship service in an evangelistic church surrounds the people with love and acceptance. Such an atmosphere comes when the power of God's Spirit works in the lives of his people. It comes when Jesus is the focus of worship, when he receives all the praise for the growth in the church.

A person cannot sit in a pew, look at the back of someone else's head, and build loving, caring relationships. He or she must have face-to-face, personal contact with people who are longing for someone to care.

Loving Christians do not ask, How do I work my way to the top? but, How do I work my way to the bottom? Evangelistic Christians seek the role of servants; they consciously choose to wash feet. They open doors of fellowship instead of defending turf.

Such openness begins in the leadership of the church. Leaders must be trained and qualified soul winners. They should be willing to work *with* people, not over them. Self-confidence is important, but more crucial is the leader's confidence in the power of God.

Of course, leadership does not stop with the pastor. Ephesians 4:12 says the pastor should "equip *the saints* for the work of ministry." The pastor should help lay people to dream; he or she should disciple them so that they can expand their vision for God; and he or she should challenge them to trust God for the impossible.

What's impossible, anyway? During a tour to the Kennedy Space Center, a guide explained the complex guidance system that controlled a particular rocket. The guide said that the system was activated only after the rocket had gained a certain altitude. One man asked, "Why does the guidance system wait to kick in?"

The guide answered, "You don't need any guidance if you're only sitting on the pad!"

Some churches pray for a divine vision—an

awesome dream for their future. But they are still just sitting on the pad. They think the dreams they've already received are impossible to achieve. Proverbs 24:3-4 states, "Any enterprise is built by wise planning, becomes strong through common sense, and profits wonderfully by keeping abreast of the facts" (Living Bible). Growing, evangelistic congregations set goals for themselves. Goals are developed in light of the church's statements of purpose, a clear understanding of the church's mission. When a congregation sets a goal it is taking a step of faith. It is making a statement of hope for the future. Wise planning follows this sequence:

Setting the Goals

1. *Purpose*—the church's reason for being, which forms the foundation of all its actions, plans, and activities.
2. *Vision*—a mental picture of a future event by which a local church can further accomplish God's purpose in that place.
3. *Goal*—a statement that translates the future vision into present reality. A goal is specific and measurable; it has a time frame for completion.

Reaching the Goals

1. *Strategy*—the specific activities which the church will use to accomplish its goal.
2. *Schedule*—the sequence and time in which the church will carry out its various strategies.
3. *Evaluation*—the process of measuring progress and making adjustments.

reaches out to touch people for the Lord Jesus Christ. Every phase of church life—Sunday school, worship, music ministry, youth program, singles' ministry, or any other work—is seen as an opportunity for evangelistic outreach. Every program in the church is geared to reaching people for Christ, leading them to receive Christ as their Savior, teaching them to serve him as Lord.

Merely thinking about evangelism accomplishes nothing. The act of reaching out brings life to a congregation. Evangelism must not be delayed while the lay people strive to meet certain standards of maturity; any plan to revive the church first and then evangelize does not work. This introspective getting ready for evangelism is often a dead end. A church does not become more spiritual by gazing continually inward. To the contrary, a church becomes more spiritual as it gives itself away for Christ's sake.

Each person in the fellowship must have a burning desire to reach people for Christ or the congregation will soon resemble Typical Local Church. At Typical Church, the council bears the responsibility for evangelism. The council plans the church calendar, including annual events that highlight evangelism. The congregation welcomes periodic revivals and encourages sermons on evangelism. The people circulate prayer requests for specific friends and relatives to get saved. But if the congregation were to voice its feelings about evangelism, it probably would say, "We like evangelism. But it's not what we do best. We're better at Christian nurture and fellowship." At Typical Local Church, evangelism fades into the background.

Charles Simpson became pastor of a congregation of eighty persons in 1962, at the age of twenty. "I was a tremendous visitor," Charles says. "I visited all of our membership every two months; . . . forty would be in church on Sunday. But somehow the other forty felt free to call themselves Christians." Six years later, the congregation had about three hundred members and Charles was hospitalized with heart trouble. The doctor said he was under too much stress.

"There seemed to me to be only two options. Either the church was once what the Book of Acts said it was, in which case we were subnormal by a long shot. Or it never was what Acts said, and then I really had nothing to preach."[14]

When a church does nothing in outreach, it becomes fat and lazy. Sometimes a congregation needs to break out of traditional ways that are not working and seek new avenues of outreach. A church that stretches every muscle to fulfill the Great Commission will grow healthy and effective. The church will be so busy loving Christ and each other that it will have no time to complain. With eyes fastened on the Master's great harvest field, they will be growing a congregation with an evangelistic life-style.

Is your local church carrying the Gospel of Christ to the community? Have you discovered ways to reach people at their point of need? Have you made every effort to go beyond the confines of your building to share Christ with those who never will visit the church on their own initiative?

As a local congregation develops and grows its unique life-style of evangelism, it realizes that methods from the past may no longer be effective. Nineteenth-century revivalism is not spreading the gospel today. The Church has often oversimplified issues and diagnosed the problems of the world in terms of a single issue, such as, "We need to be more spiritual." In light of that diagnosis, the Church has advocated simple solutions, such as "Let's get back to God" or, "Christ is the answer." Each of these statements contains the truth. But we do not need to answer the call back to God so much as the call to go forward with God. God is to be found not so much in a romantic past but in the anguish and pain, the hope and joy of today's complex world.

In the following interview, pastors of working churches share their insights into a life-style of evangelism. These churches are as unique as the communities they serve. They have designed their evangelism strategy to meet the needs in their communities. Their stories are not here to offer yet more sure-fire shortcut ways to evangelize, but to stimulate you to define your community's needs and build effective life-style evangelism ministries in your own neighborhood.

What is the secret of churches on the grow? Home Bible studies; aggressive leadership; soul winning; small growth groups; biblical preaching; trained and equipped laity. What is the answer? Probably there is no wrong answer. A chief concern is that what works for one congregation at a certain location may not work exactly the same for another, without a tailoring process. What some churches don't need is just another program.

Some situations are in peril from "programitis." In some cases, it could be like asking a heart patient to do three miles around the track. This is not just a statement on programs and methods. The need is for biblical principles that lead to an evangelistic life-style. This volume will attempt to give a biblical study as well as practical applications of evangelistic ministries.

The purpose of this book is not to publicize an individual church or pastor. Rather, the hope is to show the life-style evangelistic characteristics and principles that can make any church healthy and effective, regardless of size. Some are large and some are small.

To select the congregations for a writing of this type is not an easy process. It evolved over a period of a couple of years with input from pastors, state executives, and national church leaders. A number of churches could have been included and probably should have been included, but time and writing space would not permit.

Notes

1. C. B. Hogue, *Life-Style Evangelism—Love Leaves No Choice* (Waco, Tex.: Word Books, 1976), 140.

2. Norman Cousins, quoted by Charles W. Forman, *A Faith for the Nations* (Philadelphia: Westminster Press, 1957), 51-52.

3. William F. Keucher, *Good New People in Action* (Valley Forge: Judson Press, 1975), 26.

4. Jack Hyles, *Let's Go Soul Winning* (Murfreesboro, Tenn.: Sword of the Lord, 1962), 11-12.

5. Michael Green, *Evangelism in the Early Church* (Grand Rapids: Wm. B. Eerdmans, 1970), 280.

6. Lewis Perry Chafer, *True Evangelism* (Chicago: Moody Press, 1919).

7. C. E. Autrey, *Basic Evangelism* (Grand Rapids: Zondervan, 1959), 54-55.

8. Leslie Woodson, *Evangelism for Today's Church* (Grand Rapids: Zondervan, 1973), 71.

9. T. W. Manson, *The Church's Ministry* (Philadelphia: Westminster Press, 1958), 107.

10. Andrew Murray, *Like Christ* (New York: J. H. Sears and Company, n.d.), 66.

11. Oscar E. Feucht, *Everyone a Minister* (St. Louis: Concordia Publishing House, 1974), 81.

12. Lewis A. Drummond, *Leading Your Church in Evangelism* (Nashville: Broadman Press, 1975), 59-60.

13. Carlyle Marney, *Priests to Each Other* (Valley Forge: Judson Press, 1974), 9.

14. Kevin F. Perrotta, "The Multiplication of the Pastoral Leaders" *Pastoral Renewal* (September 1981), 19.

"The pastor has to be a personal evangelist and share his enthusiasm with the people."

Chapter 1

A Soul-winning Church
Pastor Marvin Sanders

Overview

Lexington is situated in the center of Blue Grass country. The horse business and Lexington's other industries draw the unemployed from eastern Kentucky. The tobacco and coal industries, an IBM complex, North American Rockwell, Ashland Oil, and other industries offer jobs in a stable, growing economy. The University of Kentucky, Transylvania University, and Asbury College and Theological Seminary draw students and educators from around the country. High-rise apartments and skyscrapers define the skyline, and trailer parks spring up to house the people who continue to move to Lexington.

Eastland Church of God serves as suburban area on the edge of the growing industrialized section of Lexington. Begun in a basement owned by Ora Davis, the Eastland Church soon moved to a store-front building. From there the church relocated as it grew under the leadership of Charles Tarr, Willard Wilcox, and Bill Neece. Growth slowed as the church filled its buildings, one after the other. Leroy Oesch followed Bill Neece, bringing plans for building more offices and classrooms. In addition, Pastor Oesch launched the bus ministry. With room to expand, the church showed vigorous numerical and financial growth.

Calling Pastor Marvin Sanders in 1978, the church studied its options. Their morning worship attendance stood at four hundred. They could stay where they were and stagnate; they could begin a daughter congregation; or they could move to a new building designed for their specific ministry. The congregation decided to relocate to the acreage purchased under Pastor Oesch's leadership. The new facility, completed in June 1981, seats 750 and can be expanded to accommodate 1,000 in worship. A gym/multipurpose building is detached from the main facility. For the first time in a long time, Eastland Church has room to grow. In six years, their morning worship attendance has grown to 648.

People from low-income areas ride Eastland's buses and worship alongside the middle-class, blue-collar workers who make up most of the congregation. Students, primarily seminarians from Asbury, add to the church's diversity. The congregation is integrated. A singles' ministry is just getting started.

Interview

Charles: Pastor Sanders, who is Eastland Church of God?

Pastor Sanders: Eastland Church is a group of people who have a genuine love that says to black, white, upper class, lower class, educated, and uneducated, "God loves you, and Jesus Christ is the answer for the problems you face." We have people from all over the country. Our people come from different religious backgrounds, diverse cultural backgrounds, and different economic backgrounds. But one thing that comes through every group, through everything we do, is love. Our people are burdened for other people. They go out of their way to be friendly, to help others feel loved and accepted. More than anything else, we are a soul-winning church.

Charles: How do you lead your people in that direction? What is your leadership style?

Pastor Sanders: I consider myself a team man. We have a large staff, counting our part-time workers. Our weekly staff meetings are a time for planning. I meet often with the church council, keeping them aware of our plans and planting seeds so that they have time to think through an idea. I don't consider myself a dictator. I need support and backing from spiritual people I trust. I want their thinking and their involvement. If the Lord is leading me as pastor and them as lay leaders, he certainly will make all of us sensitive to his leading. Through our leaders, the Holy Spirit confirms what the church should be doing.

Charles: How do you create a positive atmosphere for evangelism? How do you make that happen?

Pastor Sanders: In my judgment, the pastor is the key. The pastor has to be a personal evangelist and share his enthusiasm with his people. The people take on the personality of the pastor. If he is warm and approachable, they will be, too. The pastor's willingness to try, to be human, even to fail, will help his people risk themselves. You can't lead people where you haven't been. So I feel the enthusiasm for evangelism rises and falls on the pastor's leadership.

Charles: What's the strategy here? How do you evangelize?

Pastor Sanders: We use the Evangelism Explosion program; we have two semesters each year. Campus Crusade's Four Spiritual Laws program first introduced me to structured soul-winning. We've used the Board of Church Extension and Home Missions program. Any program will work if people will commit themselves to it.

Charles: Do you consider bus ministry part of your strategy?

Pastor Sanders: The bus ministry opens a lot of doors. Normally bus ministry brings to mind low-income areas, and we do run our buses to those people. But we bring people from middle-class and upper-class areas as well. Several of those families have been won to Christ through the bus ministry. In many cases, we win the children first and the parents come later. One woman sent her children on the bus and finally agreed to come herself on Mother's Day. The Lord prepared her; she was the first one at the altar that day. She's a bus pastor today.

Charles: What other outreach methods do you use?

Pastor Sanders: We're beginning growth groups. And our athletic programs have brought us new people. We've seen conversions through athletics—four on our women's softball teams this year, and three on our junior high basketball team. We've had similar results in the men's program.

Charles: How many hours do your people spend in structured evangelism?

Pastor Sanders: Our E.E. teams visit every Tuesday night. Except for my own personal visitation, our only other visitation is through the bus ministry. The bus workers, twelve to twenty of them, meet every Saturday for a hefty breakfast. Then they set goals for their buses and knock on doors. Each bus captain may knock on fifty to one hundred doors. One man visits every night. He'll bring in a hundred people using two buses.

Charles: How do you recruit the people who visit?

Pastor Sanders: One on one. We don't do a lot of recruiting from the pulpit. In E.E., for instance, we enlist people with a high level of commitment. We invite them to a banquet and then lay down the terms of the E.E. covenant. Some are ready to make the commitment; others aren't.

Charles: Who are you trying to reach in your ministry? Not just the bus ministry, but with your whole outreach?

Pastor Sanders: We don't pick and choose, brother. We just go from house to house. We get leads from visitors to our services and from our own people who know someone who'd like a visit. But we also go door to door, apartment to apartment.

Charles: Why are people attracted to this congregation?

Pastor Sanders: The main attraction is our own people and their excitement about the church. And then some hear the "Christian Brotherhood Hour" and some see the special TV ministries of the church. Others come from the bus ministry or the E.E. program. But our people are the main attraction.

Charles: What about new convert incorporation? What do you do with baby Christians?

Pastor Sanders: We have a structured Christian Nurture class, twelve weeks of specialized studies. Next the new converts move to the Basic Bible class. After that, they can elect to take the Prayer class. I've wondered about the wisdom of isolating these new Christians from the rest of the church, but the system has worked well. The new converts can be involved in church life wherever they choose while they're taking the classes.

In addition, we get people established by matching each new Christian with a family or person already in the church. And the E.E. plan contains structured follow-up as well.

Charles: Do you further disciple new converts?

Pastor Sanders: We use Dr. Robert Coleman's books, *Established in the Word* and *Life in the Living Word*. We plan to establish discipleship groups as soon as we get some training. We'll use either Navigator or Churches Alive materials.

Charles: You mentioned outreach through bus work, Evangelism Explosion, the athletic program—do you have specialized ministries, the kind that require specific counseling training?

Pastor Sanders: Every Tuesday a group goes to the nursing homes. We visit in the jails, but that program isn't an organized effort.

Charles: Other than your programs, what makes Eastland successful?

Pastor Sanders: Strong lay leadership, people who mean business about being Christians. To them, it's not a game. They love the Lord and do their best for his church. Many of our board members also work in E.E. Our Sunday school superintendant is an E.E. trainer. We have people talented and gifted in music and other areas of leadership.

Charles: What's on the drawing board for your congregation?

Pastor Sanders: Continued strength in the pulpit and in our Sunday school teaching. We've been so busy with the building project, many other plans have been on the back burner. But we're planning to have teacher training this year. We also want to train altar workers and ushers. Our youth minister is developing SALT ministries, which involve satellite groups in communities where some of our young people live. The youth invite their friends to these neighborhood groups. Our youth pastor really drives home evangelism; he says he'd rather be out winning souls than having a car wash.

Charles: These plans all point to evangelism and discipling. You seem to have definite goals in mind. What principles might another church be able to incorporate into their own ministry? What concepts that you use could transfer to another congregation?

Pastor Sanders: The church must be unified. That is essential. Squabbling and friction in a church disqualify any outreach program; the Lord is not going to honor division and hostility. The church must be united in love. Second, that love must be trained. We send our people to seminars to be challenged, to learn how to channel their love into outreach. That's how we started our bus ministry. We saw the possibilities, got some training, and put what we learned into practice.

Charles: You spoke about unity. How do you unify the body of Christ?

Pastor Sanders: In large measure, it comes from the pulpit. I think in most churches there is a dearth of preaching on the Holy Spirit and his work. The Holy Spirit brings unity and the fruits of gentleness, love, joy, peace, and kindness. When I first came to Eastland, I preached for months and months on the work of the Holy Spirit. Some people got hit straight in the teeth by that kind of preaching and spun right out of the church. Other people drew together in unity and love. We refuse to be drawn into a fight. We love in spite of differences in doctrine. We love people into unity.

You can't overemphasize the Spirit. It is essential that the Holy Spirit fill people with power and boldness and love. No program can produce that. No workshop can duplicate it. So I preach and preach a definite born-again experience and a definite infilling of the Spirit. And we get people working, involved in the work of the church.

Discussion

Jesus is the first evangelist, the continuous seeker. Out of God's unchanging love, he names Christians to be co-workers with him. God calls out the Church to share in his mission of redeeming the world. The Apostle Paul boldly stated, "We are laborers together with God" (1 Cor. 3:9). And the words of the Master still ring with challenge: "As my Father hath sent me, even so send I you" (John 20:21).

1. William Temple thus defines the nature of evangelism like this: "To evangelize is so to present Christ Jesus in the power of the Holy Spirit, that people shall come to put their trust in God through him, to accept him as their Savior and to serve him as their Lord in the fellowship of his Church."* Using this definition, evaluate the work of Eastland Church and

your own congregation. Write Yes or No in each space below:

	Eastland	My Church
Does the church present Christ in the power of the Spirit?	_____	_____
Are people accepting Jesus as their Savior?	_____	_____
Are these people serving him in the fellowship of the church?	_____	_____

2. How does the story of Eastland Church challenge you? _____

_____

_____

_____

3. Many people say, "It doesn't matter what you believe as long as you believe something; so I don't try to push the gospel on someone who already has a religion." Read Colossians 1:16-20, 1 Corinthians 3:10-11, and Acts 17:30-31. In light of these scriptures, would you agree with that statement? Why or why not? _____

_____

_____

_____

4. Whom does God expect to do the work of evangelism? (Base your answer on 1 Peter 2:9-

10, John 17:20-21, and Matthew 12:33-37.)_____

_____

_____

_____

5. Read Jesus' Great Commission in Matthew
28:16-20. Some say that Jesus gave this Great
Commission only to a few Christians who receive the gift of evangelism. What do you think?

_____

_____

_____

Now read 1 John 4:13-17. Here the Bible keeps
referring to *we;* who are these people?_____

_____

_____

_____

What does the Bible say *we* do

  in verse 13?_____

  _____

  _____

  in verse 14?_____

  _____

  _____

  in verse 15?_____

_____

_____

in verse 16?_____

_____

_____

in verse 17?_____

_____

_____

What light does this scripture shed on the Great Commission? _____

_____

_____

_____

---

*Robert N. Munger, "Some Guidelines of Evangelism Tomorrow," *Journal of Theology,* Spring 1976, 40.

Chapter 2

"Our work with the
handicapped has taught us
openness."

Chapter 2
Recognize the Needs
Pastor Robert C. Preston
Jo Preston

Overview

The Newport church serves an area of fifteen thousand people. About five thousand of these people live on the outskirts of this Appalachian town. Proud and hard-working, many of them holding two jobs, the people nevertheless deal with poverty. Newport is primarily farm country, although the Van Camp cannery and some other industries provide jobs as well. The town's proximity to Gatlinburg has created some minor growth as businesses and people move from the resort area to Newport. The pastor's wife, Jo, describes the townspeople as warm and personable, loving and giving.

Echoing other pastors across the country, Pastor Preston first mentioned jobs when asked about his community's needs. Second, the area needs churches. According to Pastor Preston, if everyone in Newport got up for church on Sunday, about ten thousand would have no place to worship anywhere in town. The area needs the gospel, and the lack of churches means some needs go unmet.

The Newport First Church of God began as a Kingdom Builders work in Tennessee led by Pastor James I. Turner and his wife, Judith. The church met first in homes and then in an old Presbyterian building. Pastor Preston came to the church shortly before the Presbyterian building was scheduled by the owners for demolition. Forced to meet then in storefront settings, the church lost some credibility and rapport with the townspeople. In an area known for Pentecostalism and snake-handling, another storefront church made little impact. Townspeople saw the Newport church, in Pastor Preston's words, as "just another storefront church that wasn't going to amount to anything anyway—here today and gone tomorrow." Establishing credibility, showing the town that the Newport church had valid doctrine to preach and teach, became the focus of each building project of the church.

Beginning with forty-nine dollars, two acres, and materials salvaged from the Presbyterian building, the Newport congregation laid its plans. Lacking materials for the building they envisioned, the members first built a two-story parsonage and held services in its first level. By using quality materials and workmanship, and by making long-range plans, the church established itself in the community as a congregation committed to its goals.

Yet the congregation laid aside its building plans to concentrate on an aspect of ministry then unknown in Newport. Under God's direction, the congregation founded the Church of Special Love, a ministry to the mentally handicapped. It was this ministry that finally opened Newport to the church and allowed the church to penetrate the town. When the present facilities were built, the Church of Special Love had a voice in the building plans. The building has no steps. Even the restrooms are equipped for the handicapped. A usable, serviceable building, the church is accessible to anyone in the community. The building's design would allow the church to double its seating capacity at minimal expense.

The Newport congregation resists classification. People with money and people without money work side by side. Business people, construction workers, farmers, factory workers, and supervisors worship together. Pastor Preston attributes the congregation's unity to their growth together as a family of God.

Interview

Charles: What is the mission of this church?

Jo: To meet the needs of our people. If they're sick or in trouble, we stay with them. Because we have come through some real problems, the church has learned to stand together.

Pastor Preston: For example, we have had some

people in trouble with the law. Yet even when it came out in the paper, our people said, "We are praying for you. We want you to know that we love you no matter what happens." To me, that is the goal of the church—to meet people where they are. Looking from the outside, someone might think we tolerate a lot of "non-church" behavior. Our leadership is actually very conservative. But we don't rule out someone because he's not what we think he should be. Our door is open.

Our work with the handicapped has taught us this openness. Once we took our handicapped kids to the circus. Some of the kids were black, some had money, and some had nothing. Yet when we returned from the circus, all the kids hugged and kissed each other good-bye. It made no difference to them if one had money and another didn't. There were no feelings of inferiority. Our desire as a church ought to be to create that atmosphere of love, an atmosphere that makes Jesus visible.

Charles: Can you describe your style of leadership as pastor? Are you aggressive? Shepherding?

Pastor Preston: I am aggressive in that I've never asked my people to do anything I wasn't willing to do myself. And I believe God wants a pastor to demonstrate leadership that will not be dictated to or compromised. Yet I love my people and am concerned about them. I think the congregation should be involved in the total work of the church. So I guess our leadership is a mixture of aggressiveness and love.

Charles: What about your view, Jo? What style of leadership does Bob have?

Jo: He has authority and compassion. If he teaches a Sunday school class, the children climb up on his lap. He fixes things for people, everything from washing machines to heaters. He is a sacrificing pastor. He works hard. Part of our acceptance in Newport came because Bob works hard and isn't afraid of physical labor.

Pastor Preston: It's important to remember that our setting required a long-term ministry. We had to build a relationship with this town, and that took time. If I had stayed two years and left, and then someone else stayed two years and left, the Church of God would never have made a serious impact on Newport.

Charles: Do you see yourself as a pastor/ teacher?

Pastor Preston: More than I used to. When I first came here, I plugged leaks. I was the guy whose fingers were sore from sticking them in the dike. Many of the people in this church had been hurt, wounded, disappointed. At first, I had to do everything that got done. I took people with me on hospital and nursing-home calls, trying to help them see beyond their problems, trying to help them see the needs of the community and my concerns as pastor. Counseling and leadership development took up most of my time. Now the church is much healthier— we have a lot more people who can plug leaks. I have more time to preach the Word and teach my people through the pulpit and special classes.

Charles: So you built the viability of the Church of God in this area and established your own credibility as a leader. Now, how do you create a positive atmosphere for evangelism?

Pastor Preston: First, we help our people see that they are God's people, rescued by his grace. And we help them recognize that everyone has a soul hungry for God. This realization creates within our people a love for others. No program can substitute for that love.

Charles: What kind of evangelistic strategy do you use?

Pastor Preston: We've tried all the usual programs, but I really believe the greatest of all has been that our people recognize the needs of souls and try to win them.

Personal testimonies make the difference. Our people's testimonies say to the community, "Here is a church that loves us for ourselves and not for what we can give to them." Too many churches today seem to say, "What benefit will you be to us? If you're no benefit to us, we really don't need you." Instead, we're trying to develop the attitude that everyone is needed and worthy of love. If a person has a problem, we want to work with him, not ignore him.

For example, a woman in our church has illegitimate children. The first time I visited her, she started to tell me all the things that had happened to her. I told her I was willing to listen if she needed to talk, but I didn't want her to feel obligated to tell me. I explained that if she confessed her sins to God, that was all I needed to know. She had not been comfortable in other churches, but because she knows we accept her as forgiven by God, she is faithful here.

Another part of our evangelism strategy is the rapport we've established with our business community. The town knows we're here to minister.

Charles: Your evangelistic presence, then, is through personal contact. Does this come back to evangelism as a life-style?

Pastor Preston: Yes. We've built the church by living the love of Christ in town, on the job—wherever we are. It's the most effective way. We try to lift Christ higher than anything else. With programs, people tend to become program-minded. They evangelize out of duty rather than witness for the cause of Christ. It fails somehow. We've gone out and knocked on doors with twenty-two trained soulwinning teams. People supposedly got saved at home, but we don't see them in church. In the year we spent knocking on doors, I can recall only one person who actually became part of this church as a result. Many, many more have come because of personal, day-to-day contact.

Charles: How do you train your people for evangelism?

Pastor Preston: Constant teaching through preaching, Wednesday prayer meeting, and Bible studies. Right now we're using Robert Coleman's *The Master Plan of Evangelism.* I like the plan because it brings Jesus to the forefront.

Charles: What about purposeful, targeted evangelism? How many hours in a week do your people spend in that kind of evangelism?

Pastor Preston: We don't have that kind of program right now, other than my own visiting. I see two or three families two or three times a week. Most of my evangelism comes in meeting people day to day. I can stay at the Super Dollar Market for two hours and make more visits than if I run all over town making calls at homes.

Charles: What about regular visitation? Is that a priority?

Pastor Preston: Regular visitation is a high priority in my mind, but I've not been able to get the program going like I want it. Our teachers visit their classes, and we did have the trained teams. Right now we're restructuring our whole program as we gear up to fill this new building.

Charles: What kind of people do you want to fill it with? Who are you trying to reach?

Pastor Preston: Everybody, and I don't say that as a cop-out. Many churches prepare themselves for the middle-class. The very wealthy are neglected because perhaps we feel inferior to them. The very poor are neglected because perhaps we feel a bit better. Our goal here is to reach from one end of the spectrum to the other. We minister to rich and poor, black and white.

Jo: And we minister to all denominations. As we said in an earlier conversation, only three people in our church have Church of God backgrounds. In this area, people are familiar with Pentecostalism. The Church of God is unfamiliar to these people, and every person who comes in is a brand-new experience for us.

Charles: What draws people here?

Pastor Preston: As we mentioned before, the Church of Special Love built a bridge to this community. In fact, we're known better as the Church of Special Love than as the First Church of God. The love we've shown in this ministry to the handicapped attracts other people as well.

Charles: When persons are attracted here and then make a decision for Christ, what do you do with them? How are they taught?

Pastor Preston: When anyone is saved, no matter his age, I bring him into my class to learn sound doctrine. First, I begin with what doctrine is. Because we deal with people of different denominational backgrounds, doctrine carries a certain stigma, and people often reject it. After we establish what doctrine is as we see it, then we teach what sin is and how it affects our lives.

After that, we look at salvation and day-to-day growth. It's an informal class, an open class. We encourage people to ask questions even if they think those questions are foolish. The class meets in my study, so all my reference books are right at hand. I prepare lessons for the students to work on at home, and we discuss them in class. The class runs until I think people are ready to leave; the average stay is about one year. That's how we build most of our people into Church of God doctrine. I don't preach a lot of doctrine from the pulpit, but we teach it. And more than that, we teach people to make up their own minds based on the Word of God, not just on our doctrine.

Charles: How do you disciple new Christians in the church?

Pastor Preston: We teach them and then we help them become active in the life of the church. Our Wednesday programs and Tuesday Bible studies are geared toward teaching our people to care about other people.

Charles: You've talked about the Church of Special Love. How did that ministry happen, and what other specialized ministries do you have?

Pastor Preston: If you remember, we had difficulty establishing our credibility with the people of Newport. We had begun our building program and had developed long-range goals, but God seemed to direct us away from building and into this care for the mentally handicapped. We had one handicapped boy, Joey, in our church, and his mother had carefully taught him about Jesus. We realized that many boys and girls like Joey would never get that training at home and that the church was not equipped to train them either. And we began to see that because handicapped children had no place to worship, entire families did not attend church. We didn't have any formal training, so we talked with Special Education teachers, read everything we could find on the subject, and prayed. I found that the key to this specialized ministry is not necessarily a qualified teacher, but rather people who have the love of God in their hearts and are willing to give themselves.

Besides the Church of Special Love, we are involved in the Douglas Adult Cooperative, a nonprofit program that trains eighty to eighty-five men and women who have never been to school. We work with the police department and hospitals as chaplain and lend support to various clubs. We run buses every Sunday and have a radio ministry. We also try to work with the area ministerial association, although we don't always agree on doctrine.

Charles: Why is this congregation successful? You've mentioned the specialized ministries, but what are the intangibles?

Pastor Preston: Adaptability. We are willing to adapt to this community and its needs. Second, we take a doctrinal stand that is different from every other church in the area. We are probably the only amillennial church in Newport and one of the few that doesn't practice tongues. We are not dogmatic about our doctrine; we try to present our view and then let people make up their minds. I don't back down when I'm preaching from the pulpit about issues such as the millennium and tongues, but people are not offended because they know we want them to decide for themselves.

Charles: Bob, share some concepts from your ministry that might be helpful to other congregations.

Pastor Preston: I heard Robert Schuller say that the needs of the community should determine the goals of the church. Without being quite that cut-and-dried, I basically believe that is what the church should do. We need to take a good, long look at the community we serve before we plan our programs. And from time to time we need to review the needs. We realize that everyone needs to be saved and have a church home, but beyond those needs are needs unique to each community. The Church must deal with those needs as well.

The whole concept of Christianity and the Church is to touch people's lives. It is one thing to preach unity and quite another to practice it. It is one thing to talk about the love of God, and quite another to show that love. The Church needs to say to the community, "We love you; we're not here to take something from you but to give you Jesus Christ." If ministering like that means programs for the blind, the handicapped—whatever—then we want to do it. And we leave the results up to God.

Another important concept is to help people grow after they accept Jesus. We need to develop a pastor/people relationship that will encourage growth. We involve our people in the planning, in the dreaming. We planned a meal and called it "Share Your Dreams for North Night." It was a night for brainstorming. In advance, we mailed out a sheet that listed all the things we had heard people wish for the church. We asked our people to pray about them, study them, and then to list them in order of priority. Then the entire congregation came together to discuss them. It was a rich time. The specific plans for beginning our bus ministry came out of that "Share Your Dreams" meal.

Charles: If you could summarize in one paragraph the greatest thrust of this church, what would you say?

Pastor Preston: It's hard to separate the parts of our work here. Personal witness is important, and the bus ministry provides prime prospects for us, but neither of those is the one thing that spurred our growth. Everything works together here. We involve our people and meet needs. And there is a sense of rejoicing here. In the early days when someone went to the altar, our lay leaders would look at their watches and just sigh at the long time we were taking. Now some of those people have left, and we are better for it. But some have gotten involved in other people's lives and needs, and they don't watch their watches anymore. Now there's rejoicing.

Editor's Note: Charles Moore is now pastor of First Church. In a recent interview, Pastor Moore said that a key to the future growth of the church will be "individual families who have influence." If we continue meeting the needs of people in this community, I believe our people will spread the word of what the church is doing. Word-of-mouth advertising is the best kind, you know!

"We're just trying to reach average, common people," Pastor Moore continued. "We do have special events such as a Thanksgiving auction and a Homecoming celebration each spring.

But special events are not the key to long-term growth. We need to minister to people's hurts every week, through a strong pulpit ministry, a consistent Sunday school effort, and visitation.

"First Church has real love for people," he says. "We demonstrate that love. We feel it. And we act on it. You can see it in the action of our people who respond to any need—financial or whatever—both inside the church and outside. A community cannot ignore a church with love."

We asked Pastor Moore whether First Church will continue the Church of Special Love.

"Definitely," he said. "It's one good way that we can show our love for the people of Newport. I believe we need to find additional ways to demonstrate our special love, but this ministry is certainly a good start in that direction. I'm glad the Lord moved Brother Preston to begin this program."

What about their goals for the future? "First, we need to strengthen the Christian families here," Pastor Moore says. "Second, we need to develop our lay leadership. Third, we need to develop an outreach—a systematic plan for reaching the lost in Newport. And fourth, we want to bring in a full-time associate minister in evangelism and discipleship. That last goal is probably a long way off; we're not large enough to support another full-time minister yet. But I believe we will be able to do that as the church continues to grow."

Discussion

1. In the previous chapter we read the story of Eastland Church of God in Lexington, Kentucky, a church quite different from the Newport, Tennessee, church. How are these congregations different? _____

_____

_____

_____

How are they similar? _____

_____

_____

_____

2. Pastor Preston says, "Looking from the outside, someone might think we tolerate a lot of nonchurch behavior. . . . We don't rule out someone because he's not what we think he should be." When a church holds this attitude, what are some risks that it takes? _____

_____

_____

_____

Do you believe the goal of reaching people for Christ is worth these risks?_____

_____

_____

_____

3. Pastor Preston says, "When I first came here, I plugged leaks. . . . At first, I did everything that got done. . . . Counseling and leadership development took up most of my time." Many pastors say this is common to them. How does a church get beyond this stage so that a pastor is more than just a leak-plugger of problems? _____

_____

_____

_____

4. In what ways does First Church win people to Jesus Christ? List various ways. _____

_____

_____

_____

5. God is a loving and caring God. The entire Bible reflects the assurance of 1 Peter 5:7, which says, "Cast all your care upon him; for he careth for you." As God is a loving God, his people are to become a loving people. List some things that show the people at First Church love and care for others. _____

_____

_____

_____

6. Recall an episode from Jesus' ministry in which he showed love and concern for someone.

_____

_____

_____

7. What are some ways in which your congregation could show more love and concern for the people of your community?_____

_____

_____

_____

58

Chapter 3

Our Mission: To Represent Christ
Pastor Ron Fowler

Overview

In 1968, riots ripped through East Akron. Businesses moved out, leaving the area open to prostitution, gambling, bars, and rising crime. Heavily residential, a community of older frame houses, East Akron has the lowest per capita income in Summit County.

The community has worked hard to recover. A new housing development and other new construction have helped raise property values again, and young families are moving back to the area. Middle and lower class economically, East Akron still battles its slum appearance. By staying in the community and building new facilities, Arlington Church of God spearheads a rebuilding of pride.

When asked about the needs of the East Akron community, Pastor Fowler first cites that need for pride. Because pride is blossoming, people are beginning to repair their houses, to care about their neighborhood. A second vital need is child care. Arlington's Day Care draws 60 percent of its children from mothers on welfare. Without child care services, those mothers would be unable to train for jobs. Arlington also opens its facilities to the community for voting and regular town meetings.

Young people in the community need a place to study and play, and Arlington provides The Upper Room, a coffeehouse-type meeting place. Arlington Church is sensitive to the needs of its community and has steadily supported the area through its decline and recovery.

Begun in 1917 by Pastor George Suddeth, Sr., Arlington has benefited from long pastorates. When Pastor Suddeth fell ill in 1943, the church called Pastor Fowler's father, Robert L. Fowler, who served the church until 1968. Pastor Ron Fowler assumed the pastorate in January 1969.

The Arlington Street facilities, completed in December 1980, do not quite meet the congregation's needs. Thankful for the growth that has crowded the building, Pastor Fowler now holds two worship services on Sunday mornings. With day care, a prayer circle, and senior citizens meetings, Arlington's building is in use six days every week. The congregation views this as good stewardship.

The Arlington congregation is 99 percent

black; interracial marriages have brought in the few white families. The church increasingly attracts white visitors from other parts of the city as word of the ministry spreads. Economically, the congregation is middle class with the upper- and lower-middle classes represented. In terms of social values, Pastor Fowler identifies the church as upper class.

Interview

Charles: Pastor Fowler, what is the mission of this church?

Pastor Fowler: To represent Christ in every area, in every arena of life. For example, one of our members leads a Bible study at the factory where he works. Another leads a prayer group in his office. I am grateful that believers are penetrating strategic areas of political life. Our people are catching the idea that our mission is to represent Christ wherever we are.

We want to be faithful to the Word and to share that Word on as wide a platform as we can responsibly occupy. We want to share the Word through any medium we can. We are committed to carrying his Word to as wide an audience as possible in whatever ways God makes available.

Charles: How would you describe the leadership style presented by yourself and your staff?

Pastor Fowler: We work as a team, and I see myself as the facilitator. Leadership is a democratic process here, yet the staff provides strong direction.

Charles: How is a positive climate for evangelism created here?

Pastor Fowler: It is hard for persons to feel unloved and unwanted here. This is an accepting, warm congregation. A spirit of celebration permeates the worship. Our lay leaders allow the staff to be creative, and we can dream without worrying about dollar signs. We naturally have to deal with money, but it doesn't stifle our dreaming. The congregation is willing to follow the leadership here as we believe God directs us, and we can depend on a core of people who devote time and energy to this ministry.

Charles: So this positive atmosphere comes from vision of leadership and the warmth of worship?

Pastor Fowler: And from the strength of our music ministry. It's intangible, something people have to be here to experience. Joy permeates the church because the Spirit is here with us. Our people *want* others to come here, and that openness helps new people feel accepted.

Charles: What's your strategy for evangelism?

Pastor Fowler: We consistently hold revivals and we sponsor seminars on family life each fall and spring. We canvass the neighborhood and we hold home Bible studies and prayer cells.

Charles: Is regular visitation a high priority?

Pastor Fowler: Visitation is part of our strategy. Our minister of visitation coordinates a team of people gifted in visiting and counseling. The team touches base with people in the hospital, shut-ins, and people in prison. Our prison ministry is significant; a team of four lay people goes to a county jail every Friday. I preach once a month, but it's that faithful team who really ministers at the jails.

Charles: How do you recruit these visitors?

Pastor Fowler: We sent out a call for those who felt gifted of God to minister at a bedside, person to person. These people, five in all, work with the minister of visitation. They serve communion and take tapes to people who can't attend church, and faithfully keep in contact with those people.

Charles: What about your own visitation as pastor?

Pastor Fowler: In the last couple of years, most of my contact has been with contractors and others involved in our building program! That will change now that the building is finished. And I have always kept in touch with our congregation. I call them, and if I travel I'll send some postcards to let people know I'm thinking of them and praying for them.

Charles: Are your people involved in any specialized ministries besides the jail ministry you mentioned earlier? Do you have a bar ministry, for instance?

Pastor Fowler: No, we don't have a bar ministry. We got rid of the bars; they needed to be removed from the community. Our choir does have a ministry to rest homes. Once a month during their regular rehearsal time, the choir sings for the residents. The choir loves it, and they carry the church outside the walls. For many of those shut-in folks, that's the only church they have.

Another specialized ministry might be unique to our church. God has given one woman a ministry to the bereaved. If there's a death in a family, this woman literally takes over. She handles the food, answers the phone, receives flowers, serves meals to the family, cleans the house. She doesn't stay overnight, but she comes early in the morning and stays until the family goes to bed. The staff ministers to the family until after the burial. One man in our church lost a son recently. The family had only been in our church about nine months and the man said they had never experienced the kind of love this woman gave to him and his family.

Charles: You twice made the statement, "We are going to reach this city for Christ." Who is Arlington Church of God trying to reach?

Pastor Fowler: Anyone who has shown an interest, regardless of race or economic status.

Charles: Why do people come here? What's attractive to them about this church?

Pastor Fowler: The quality of things that happen here. The attitude of the people here and their genuine enthusiasm for the church and for me as their leader. That enthusiasm is contagious! Many people come to hear me preach and many come for the excellent music service, but the climate, the quality, and the worship they experience keep them coming back.

Enthusiasm for Arlington spreads by word of

mouth. We'll advertise special events but week after week, word gets around that if you want a good worship experience, come to Arlington. Our people are growing in their own experiences, and there is no substitute for the excitement generated by personal growth.

Charles: When people accept Christ here, how do you get them growing?

Pastor Fowler: The first thing we do with new converts is learn from them. It's interesting to ask a new Christian, "What took you so long?" We can learn a lot about what we unintentionally did wrong in our witnessing. For example, one man told me he waited a long time to come to the altar because he felt we coerced new converts into saying something before the church, and he said he didn't have anything to say. We realized we were encouraging people to make statements far beyond their experience. They only mimicked others. When we stopped that coercion, people felt the freedom to come to Christ. The response amazed us. So we learn from our new converts, first of all. They help us see how non-Christians perceive the church.

Of course, we teach the new converts. We steer them into a series of three classes. The first class deals with basics of Christian faith, what the church expects of new members, and what the new members can expect of our church. The second class focuses on the Church of God and its history and heritage. The third class is devoted to developing new members into leaders. The entire series takes a year to complete. One of our elders, a man whom God has given the gift of teaching, teaches the class for new converts.

Charles: What kind of discipling method do you use?

Pastor Fowler: I mentioned our elders. We chose these twelve men for their spiritual qualities, their wisdom, and their good rapport with the people. We assign elders to new converts. No elder is responsible for more than three people at any one time. That way no one gets lost when he comes into the church. The elders are responsible to see that the new Christian attends church regularly and that he gets into the new converts' classes. The elder monitors the new Christian's spiritual growth, serves as an enabler, offers his shoulder for the new person to lean on. Many people will develop their own relationships with others in the church, and our elders are not threatened by that. But the elder still is responsible to keep up with the new convert, to make contact at least once a week.

Charles: How do you prepare these elders and other leaders for their responsibilities? I know you spend time in leadership development.

Pastor Fowler: Leadership development is number one in our strategy. We set up workshops that continuously remind our leaders of our purpose—to attract people and minister to them. If the leaders don't model that concern, the followers won't catch it.

Charles: In earlier conversations, I got the impression that you don't just talk about strategy in your meetings, but that you spend time studying the Word. Explain why you spend twenty minutes in study when you only have an hour to meet. After all, leaders are supposed to have their own study time.

Pastor Fowler: The spark that excites and stimulates believers is a sound knowledge of God's purpose in Jesus Christ. That knowledge comes from the Word. As our leaders grow in understanding the Word, they are better equipped to proclaim it. The Scripture says that as the Word increased, disciples were added. That is where evangelism must find its thrust. We must increase our leaders' ability to articulate the gospel.

If leaders can sense that an idea isn't my pet project, if they believe an idea comes from divine revelation instead of human impulse, they can grasp God's marching orders for themselves. That is why I begin every meeting with a look at a biblical passage that may add light to the project we're considering.

Charles: Other than programming, what makes this church successful?

Pastor Fowler: Beyond all our programming, and even beyond our emphasis on the Bible, our church is successful because of the personal touch. There is no substitute for it. Our church has captured the spirit of expending themselves for others. Sometimes a member will call me to say he's helped a person as much as he can help, and he'll ask me to take over. I appreciate working with our people that way. The personal touch has come from me to the leaders, because that's where I've spent my time. But in turn, the leaders touch members of the Body, and members touch each other.

Charles: Do you spend a lot of time with these leaders?

Pastor Fowler: Oh, yes. I'll have breakfast with at least two of them almost every week. We talk together and dream together. We sound out ideas before they come to the council. It took five years to build up that kind of trust with the leaders. I grew up in this congregation and perhaps that explains why we took so long to establish trust. But I think it takes more time to build trust than most people are willing to invest. I'll never forget the year when I realized that people were beginning to perceive me as their pastor. People unburdened themselves to me, confessed things they'd carried alone a long time. People found wholeness and learned to cope with their problems. When they trusted me with those kinds of problems, I knew I was leading. But it took five years.

Charles: How did you help the leaders to see themselves as leaders?

Pastor Fowler: I modeled a nondefensive leadership style to them, which invited them to share their ideas and to disagree with me. Then we held intentional planning sessions. We studied Elton Trueblood's *The Company of the Committed,* helping the leaders understand what it means to be committed to the cause of Jesus

Christ. And understanding that commitment helped us understand our commitment to each other—my commitment to them and their commitment to me as their leader. We built a lot of esteem for each other.

Charles: What principles have you established that you might transfer to another congregation?

Pastor Fowler: Number one, being faithful to a consistent study of God's Word. We let the Word inform us through worship as well as through study. Number two, we developed a core of leaders and built a high degree of trust. That trust allows us to criticize our program if necessary and still maintain our love for each other. Coupled with that is an abiding loyalty to the pastor. I don't bark about that loyalty, but it *is* part of building a significant team. Number three, we understand who we are theologically. We exist here as part of the family of God to minister to people on behalf of Christ. And we have got to be open to whomever God allows us to touch. That keeps us from being cliquish and elitist. Both tendencies can destroy the fellowship. We simply are part of the family of God.

And last, but not least, our congregation has compassion for people. They have seen that we exist to serve. From the church secretary to the janitor, from every usher right through the staff to every Sunday school teacher, we make sure we know that we're here to serve, not to be served.

Discussion

1. Read 2 Corinthians 9:10-12. Then see if you can explan why Pastor Fowler says, "We can dream without worrying about dollar signs."

_____

_____

_____

2. Pastor Fowler says, "The first thing we do with converts is learn from them." What are some things you'd like to learn from the new converts at your church? _____

_____

_____

_____

3. Review the work of an *elder* in the New Testament church (Acts 15:22-23; Titus 1:5-9; 1 Pet. 5:1-3). How do Arlington's elders fit this Bible pattern?_____

_____

_____

_____

4. Pastor Fowler spends much of their committee time in Bible study—about twenty minutes of Bible study in an hour-long committee meeting. Why?_____

_____

_____

_____

5. How much Bible study do your boards
and committees do before they make decisions?

_____

_____

"We advertise programs that would appeal to the community."

Chapter 4

Putting the Unchurched
Ahead of the Churched

Pastor Raymond Cotton

Overview

A city of about 27,000 people, Wichita is based on industry. Growth is slow and steady, and the 3 percent unemployment rate falls well below the national average. Corporations seek to bring new families to the city to meet the demand for skilled workers, but high interest rates prevent those families from buying homes. About 8 percent of Wichita's population is Hispanic; about 20 percent is black.

Central Community Church is located in downtown Wichita just off the area's major highway. Most of the people in the area are single, and most rent their homes. Per capita income here ranks below the city average. A declining neighborhood, the area around Central Community Church generally is lower-middle class.

Pastor Ray Cotton lists family concerns first when discussing the needs of the Central Church community. Divorce cripples many of the families in the area, and so counseling takes high priority in his ministry. Other families need financial counseling in a tight economy. Pastor Cotton notes an increase in the number of people who come to the church for help with depression or problems with their children. Particularly in families hurt by divorce, children exhibit emotional and discipline problems that overwhelm their burdened parents. Central Community Church feels keenly its obligation to offer healing to families.

Central Community Church was established in 1907, but experienced little real growth until Pastor E. E. Kardatzke came as pastor in 1942. By the 1950s the church had grown enough to sponsor four daughter churches in Wichita. By 1965, the church had built a new sanctuary, welcomed a new pastor, Marvin Baker, and reached its highest average attendance, about four hundred. The new pastor stayed three years and was followed by another pastor, Kenneth Tabor, who stayed about five years. Pastor Cotton joined Pastor Tabor's staff in early 1974, becoming senior pastor when Pastor Tabor left in September of that year. Under Pastor Cotton's leadership, the church has increased its attendance to one thousand. Although the congregation now holds double worship services and Sunday school hours, the facilities probably cannot accommodate the growth rate for more than two more years. The leadership currently is studying several expansion possibilities.

Central Church draws its congregation from low- to upper-middle-class white people, the majority of them young middle-class families. Nearly 180 people of the congregation are children five years old and younger. No ethnic groups are represented in the congregation.

Interview

Charles: What do you see as the church's mission here in Wichita?

Pastor Cotton: Seven years ago we sat down and decided what we were going to do and how we were going to do it. Our primary goal is to win people to Jesus Christ. Our method for doing that is to meet people's needs. That's the philosophy we've developed.

Charles: Ray, how would you describe your style of leadership, especially with reference to your position as senior pastor?

Pastor Cotton: I've given some thought to that. I feel I'm a coach working with a team to get the job done. When I first came here, we had a lot of strong lay people with underdeveloped potential. Our first task involved helping those people find and develop their ministries. We help our people feel the importance of their ministries; they know what they're doing is vital, not just church busy work. We have capable people. I feel comfortable with their lay leadership.

I see myself as the leader of this congregation, the one in front setting the example. I have the vision, and yet I don't see myself as the boss. I encourage my staff to develop their strengths.

Charles: You've obviously developed your leadership here. How do you create a positive climate for evangelism in the church?

Pastor Cotton: First of all, it has to come from the pastor, from the pulpit. We all say we want to reach people for Christ, but bringing in new people upsets the status quo; I don't think some people are so open to growth as they think they are. So first we approached evangelism from the biblical standpoint, to find out what the Bible says about our priorities.

Then, I started sharing this idea with our leadership group. I talked with the leaders I thought were open to it—sharing that dream of being an evangelistic church. Then I met with small groups of leaders at retreats and in evening coffee groups, setting goals and sharing my vision. We started translating goals and priorities into practical steps for making evangelism a life-style, a reality. Once the goal was set, we began to expose our people to evangelism seminars and to books. I would take one or two lay leaders with me to seminars or give a leader a book to read, and then he would share it with the rest of the congregation. We used Sunday school campaigns to encourage people to bring their friends. Now our people live evangelism every day, and they bring their friends without any special campaigns. The evangelistic life-style has permeated the life of the church.

Charles: Do you have a specific strategy for evangelism?

Pastor Cotton: Our strategy calls for people to share with their friends, neighbors, and families what Christ is doing in their lives. And they share the help and resources they have found through the church. People get saved in several different places—in Sunday morning worship services, in homes where relationships have been built, in our offices. We steer newcomers to our small-group Bible studies and they get saved there. We don't have a set plan for the small groups. At any given time, we might have a women's group, a singles' group, and some that are not organized by the church but are people who just decided to get together.

Charles: What about training? Do you have a regular training program for personal evangelism?

Pastor Cotton: No, although we really considered it. We've participated in mass evangelism in the city, such as "Here's Life, America" and the Leighton Ford crusade. Those mass programs have not added families to the local church, but our people have benefited from the training. I have done a Sunday night series on leading people to Christ. We plan to include more training in our new discipling program.

One of the principles we use is Robert Schuller's idea of putting the needs of the unchurched ahead of the churched. There's nothing in our church that doesn't have an evangelistic focus. We've tried to permeate the church with the vision of the needs beyond the church.

Charles: Would you say regular visitation is a high priority?

Pastor Cotton: Not really. We do follow up on new people who come in, but we usually call them or someone will ask them to dinner. We really haven't had to use regular visitation.

Charles: Who is Central Community Church trying to reach? People from the downtown area or of a certain economic bracket?

Pastor Cotton: First, we're out to reach everyone that we can reach for Christ. Within that context, we realize there are certain people we can reach more effectively than others. We know we're most effective with singles and middle- to upper-middle-class families.

Charles: Why do new people come to church here? What attracts them to your congregation?

Pastor Cotton: The major attraction is people sharing with people. Our people talk with others on the job, in their neighborhoods, in their families. No other method even comes close to that one-on-one sharing. It's been the source of our growth. The Sunday school campaigns I mentioned helped get the growth cycle started, but our people are effective witnesses now because they're excited about Christ, not just because we're running a campaign.

And we catch the community's attention with advertising. We advertise heavily at Christmas and Easter when people think about church. We advertise programs that would appeal to the community, such as Family Enrichment and Singles' Seminars. Most churches advertise on the church page, but the only people who read the church page are church people. So we'll place an ad in the sports section if we're having a sports star speaker. We'll advertise a family seminar in the entertainment section. And we don't push the church up front. We catch the readers' attention by appealing to their need. For a Family Enrichment Seminar, the ad might start with the headline, "Are you getting the most out of your marriage?" Then at the bottom of the ad, we'll put the church name. The important thing is not the church but the need we're trying to meet.

Charles: People come to church for various reasons, but they stay for basically two reasons: they meet God and they make friends. How do you help people make friends here?

Pastor Cotton: Sunday school plays a key role. People in a Sunday school class automatically are part of a small group within the church. In our classes that are growing, we have "minglers" whose sole responsibility is to help people get acquainted. We train the minglers, and we provide coffee and doughnuts to encourage people to stand around and talk. We started with a class that was averaging about seventy. The teacher and I worked to set up smaller groups within that class—socials and parties—to get people acquainted. The class grew to 250 and then we split it and started over. Other classes work more toward education and nurturing, but we encourage them to be evangelistic, too.

Charles: Besides helping new people make friends, how do you deal with new converts?

Pastor Cotton: We run a pastor's class four times a year, and we encourage new converts to join a small group Bible study. We try to team them one on one with a stronger Christian, but that isn't an organized effort. We plan to set up classes that take new Christians through four or five steps of basic teaching. That program is just getting underway.

Charles: Is discipling part of your plan?

Pastor Cotton: We're starting a series of nurturing and discipling classes, but most of our discipling comes by teaming new Christians with stronger Christians. We're looking for models in this area; we really don't have the program we want to have.

Charles: Is the church involved in specialized ministries of outreach? The kind of ministry that requires special training such as for jail ministry or bar ministry?

Pastor Cotton: Our singles work is our largest specialized ministry, and even that has subdivisions. Some people have never been married. Some have struggled with divorce. Some are widowed. The needs differ within each group. We work to get the singles supporting each other, taking care of each other.

Then we have classes and activities for the mentally handicapped. We don't just meet them at church, either; we host community-wide seminars on various topics for the handicapped. Our first seminar dealt with dying and grief because we discovered that most mentally handicapped people are sheltered from death and don't know how to cope with it. After that, we planned a seminar on health, hygiene, grooming, and appearance. The couple who lead the handicapped ministry give the city leadership in this area, too. We see the church starting to carry the weight of some work affected by the Reagan budget cuts.

Our Care Program, another special ministry, covers five areas: hospital visitation, shut-in visitation, transporation for people who need rides, prayer chain, and food for people who need help. We've expanded the Care Program by enrolling thirty-five to forty of our people in the Stephen's Ministry, a fifty-hour training program that spans six months. The students learn to counsel those who are depressed and grieving (because of death or loss). Then they commit to serving as a Stephen's Minister for two years. Our Stephen's Ministers will do our hospital visitation, along with the pastors.

Other people in our Care Program send cards to people in the hospital, to those who are grieving, and to those working through a difficult problem. Many times the people writing cards don't even know who they're writing to—but people respond to the cards sometimes for that very reason. A card from someone in the church can say, "We don't know you yet, but we love you already, and we care that you're going through this difficult time."

Charles: What has made this church successful? What concepts have you used here that another church could use?

Pastor Cotton: First, decide what your church is about. What is the church really supposed to do? Every church must know its goals and responsibilities. That comes from the Bible. The Bible mandate gives the church its flame, its fire. We're an evangelistic church; our responsibility is to reach our community for Christ.

Next, I think the church has to understand the needs of its community. Once a church recognizes its area's needs, it can meet them. Without spending another dollar, the church can rearrange some priorities, eliminate some other programs, reallocate money already budgeted. Then they can evaluate the needs they see and choose where to start. As the church anticipates more money, staff, and programming, they can meet other needs, expand their vision. I think any church will grow if it's meeting the needs of people.

Another important thing is fellowship. When people come into church, they should be able to make friends with the people here. We have fellowship times before Sunday school with coffee and doughnuts. We have lots of dinners—class dinners, workers' dinners, carry-ins, and so on. We also have after-church fellowships on Sunday nights. I really encourage my people to have fellowship. I think that when a church closes its kitchen, that's a bad sign; it shows the people don't care for each other. People like to get together and make new friends. These fellowship times let them do that.

Charles: Describe Central Community Church, Ray. What happens when people worship here.

Pastor Cotton: We have an open altar in our worship services. Sometimes we invite people to pray at the altar during the morning prayer, instead of just at the end of the service. Sometimes we make microphones available during services, and people share what the Lord is doing in their lives. There is warmth and expectancy and a kind of spiritual celebration in our church.

Discussion

1. Pastor Cotton says he uses the principal of "putting the needs of the unchurched ahead of the churched." How has this congregation done that?_____

_____

_____

_____

Do you believe this is a valid, Bible-based principle? _____

_____

_____

_____

2. How does the Wichita church follow up with people who visit its services? _____

_____

_____

_____

3. List several ways in which they reach new people: _____

_____

_____

_____

4. What groups of people does the church aim to reach with special ministries? _____

_____

_____

_____

5. When Pastor Cotton described their worship services, he said, "There is warmth and expectancy and a kind of spiritual celebration in our church." What aspects of your worship services show that same kind of attitude? _____

_____

_____

_____

What might you do differently in your worship service to enhance the attitude of "expectancy and celebration?"_____

_____

_____

_____

6. Read how the Bible describes the first church that the Lord established (Acts 2:41-47).

List ways in which the Wichita congregation resembles that church: _____

_____

_____

_____

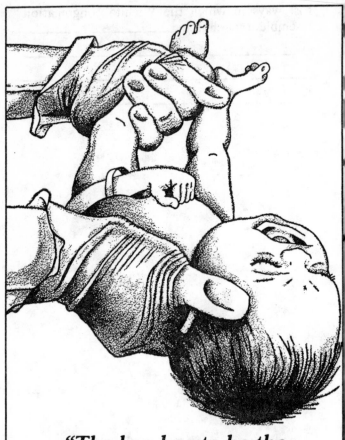

"The key has to be the reality of Jesus Christ in a person's life to the point that witnessing is as natural as breathing."

Chapter 5

It's as Natural
as Breathing
Pastor John Boedeker

Overview

First Church of God in Dallas serves a changing neighborhood on the southwest side of the city. The "white flight" trend has reversed and white families are moving back into the area, evenly balancing the neighborhood among whites, blacks, and Hispanics.

Dallas is an aggressive city, drawing people from around the country to its business community. Many of the newcomers are single and in need of companionship and fellowship. First Church recognizes their loneliness and ministers to them. Evangelism takes high priority as the church sees people burdened with low self-esteem, not knowing they are "fearfully and wonderfully made" by God. Families in turmoil inflict a 50 percent divorce rate on Dallas, and the church counters with the gospel and counseling. Drug abuse presents the church with many opportunities for ministry. Families, especially blacks and Hispanics, have been wounded by the sluggish economy and senior adults need help in understanding the legal and social services available to them. The church involves itself in the needs of these people.

First Church began its ministry in 1914 as a storefront church in southeast Dallas. By the early 1920s the church had grown enough to build its first building. As it grew to about one hundred in attendance, the congregation envisioned a steadily growing church with expanding ministries and built again in 1970. Pastor Boedeker came in 1977. The church recently completed a youth and educational facility and modified the existing building to better use that space. The church views its facilities and its plans to expand those facilities as tools for advancing the kingdom of God. Dollars spent for bricks are dollars spent for changed lives. At this time the church has not seen the will of God concerning relocation.

First Church people come from all parts of Dallas, although most live in the southwest section. Sixty to 70 percent live in Duncanville, a thriving suburb six miles from the church. Church members generally are middle- to upper-middle class. Many of the people are professionals, typical of southwest Dallas. Some black and Hispanic families attend. Most of the congregation are young families with small children and teen-agers, or elderly people, those over seventy-five. Comparatively few fall in the fifty-five to seventy-five age group. The present morning worship attendance averages more than 466.

Interview

Charles: Can you describe your present style of leadership?

Pastor Boedeker: I see myself as a servant of the people. If people see servanthood demonstrated they'll believe and follow the leadership God calls me to give. I believe in leadership based on spiritual gifts. God has given me the gift of exhortation. He's gifted others of our staff with teaching. And we look beyond the staff to the laity and their gifts to build a shared ministry. The staff members don't see themselves as assistants to the pastor but as ministers called of God to a complete responsibility. We coordinate our work, but they're free to establish their own styles of ministry. So I do not see myself as the boss of this church. I see myself as one of the people God has gifted in this place. My major leadership thrust is developing other people. After my personal relationship with God and my relationship with my family, my top priority is building up leaders in a one-on-one discipling ministry.

When I first came here, I found a congregation open to God's plans for them. They wanted the New Testament concept of lay ministry but didn't know how to get there. In the past, they had expected the pastor to do the things that God began to show them are their responsibility: *they* were to be witnesses; *they* were to seek and develop spiritual gifts, *they* were to be discipled and to disciple others. In fact, when I came I spoke with the seven-member pulpit committee and found each one ready to be discipled and equipped. They followed through on those desires, and their growth is exciting.

Right now we are moving toward establishing an eldership as patterned by the New Testament. As the Holy Spirit leads us, we should be able to agree 100 percent on the decisions made as a leadership team.

Charles: How is a positive atmosphere for evangelism created here?

Pastor Boedeker: The heart of Jesus is evangelistic. If people have the reality of Jesus Christ in their lives, if his heart reaches out through them, they'll be motivated to evangelize. Even my own personal desire to obey God isn't enough motivation. I need the heart of Jesus, the heart that wept over Jerusalem and that sees without prejudice. People need more than external motivation. Consider Campus Crusade's Four Spiritual Laws. They can organize people and send them out to knock on doors in controlled circumstances, but take away the circumstances and the witness stops. The key has to be the reality of Jesus Christ in a person's life and growth toward Christlikeness to the point that witnessing is as natural as breathing. You can't help witnessing if you're abiding in the vine.

Charles: How do you help that growth happen? How do you help people abide in the vine?

Pastor Boedeker: Everything we do inside this building is aimed at that. This is the equipping station. From the smallest child to the oldest adult, we encourage people to grow and seek and hunger and thirst for Christian living. Pulpit ministry, teaching ministry, discipleship ministry, Bible studies—whatever we do must aim for the goal of Christlikeness, or we stop doing it.

Charles: What is your basic evangelistic strategy?

Pastor Boedeker: Relational evangelism. Teaching people to build relationships and to serve. Relational evangelism is a way-of-life witness on the job, in the community, or wherever we can build relationships with unbelievers. Most of our teaching comes through small group Bible studies, in which people learn the principles of friendship evangelism. It also comes through Evangelism Explosion, where people learn to share their faith. On Thursday nights, the evangelism teams visit everyone who comes to this church. But Evangelism Explosion is not an end in itself; if it were, we'd stop this week. The program is only a tool to use as people begin to witness as a way of life and to train others to witness.

Charles: In regard to the total ministry of this church, how many hours per week do you spend in purposeful evangelism?

Pastor Boedeker: I see everything we do in that

light. Our compelling reason for existence is to glorify God. We focus on three ways to do that: one, worship him in spirit and truth; two, grow in Christ; and three, reach unbelievers with the gospel. The three really can't be separated because as we worship, we grow, and as we grow, we witness. So I say 100 percent of our work is evangelism; even a social activity is part of the body life that helps people see Christ's love in action. I don't mean to imply that we've reached our best in evangelism. We have a long way to go. But evangelism is the only reason I've not been taken to heaven. I could praise and worship better there. But I can evangelize only here.

Charles: Is regular visitation a high priority?

Pastor Boedeker: Visitation lets people know we care about them. As I said, we visit everyone who comes to this church. Visitation tells people we care who they are. From that standpoint visitation is important, but I don't think that's the way we'll win our community.

Charles: What do you see as a more viable way to win people?

Pastor Boedeker: Ministering daily in our unique arenas of relationship. Right now on the drawing board is a design for small groups that will operate geographically. They will militantly evangelize in their separate areas. They will bring new people from their areas into these groups, disciple them, and then divide and start again. These groups will be very much like the home churches of the New Testament.

Charles: Who are you trying to reach?

Pastor Boedeker: Every single person with whom we have contact. Black, white, yellow, red, rich, poor—I don't see that Christ died for some but not for others. I know statistics prove that we minister within cultures, that we reach people most like ourselves. Yet I think that is the shame of Christians. He wants us to have such oneness that things that would divide us don't divide us at all. Some of our folks still struggle with cultural hang-ups, but this church really opens its arms to anyone. Anything less quenches the Spirit of Christ.

Charles: Why are people attracted to First Church?

Pastor Boedeker: Our people are excited. I would like to think they're more excited about Jesus than about this fellowship in particular. I would like to think people are attracted to Jesus, not necessarily to First Church.

Some new families come for our youth discipleship program. And people here are excited about worship. When I came, the fellowship followed the standard evangelical pattern: prayer at a certain time and just this many hymns, with the numbers announced three times so nobody made a mistake. We've progressed. The Lord has allowed us to begin to understand what worship really is. Our understanding probably has grown from our private worship. Worship is more than singing songs; it is meeting God. God is our audience. People are performers. Those on the platform merely prompt. Our worship is a time of God's presence, of his power. Some people want more excitement in worship and try charismatic worship, but they feel manipulated by emotionalism. They come here and find balance. We want God's sovereignty and eminence, but we want a warm spirit of praise as well. People have tried to worship God with just their minds, not allowing their spirits to worship. Praising with mind and spirit together unleashes power in the church.

Charles: I sense love and warmth here that is more than feeling or something put on.

Pastor Boedeker: Over the past six months we've studied the love commandments—the "one anothers." The Lord has used that study to develop a new awareness of our oneness. We're learning to serve one another, forgive one another, forbear one another. The Holy Spirit has poured love and unity into our fellowship.

And I think God cares more about the way I treat my brother than about the way I treat him. By that I mean that God is big and can stand even my hostile reactions, but my brothers and sisters are vulnerable and might not stand up so well without love and care. We love to come together to praise and worship, but if that praise doesn't come to life in the way I treat my brother, it's the hollow emotion of the Pharisees. Our people are learning to share their possessions, too.

For example, one family needed nine hundred dollars at the last minute as they were buying a house. They asked their Bible study group to pray. They sought to know whether God was closing a door. They certainly didn't ask for money. But the next Sunday the group gave them nine hundred dollars.

In another case, a young black pastor in Dallas is building a church, and our church gave him seven hundred dollars to meet a need in his family. Our people do put their treasures where their hearts are. They're generating a lot of love. We're progressing here. We're not perfect, but we're struggling in some beautiful areas of growth.

Charles: What do you do with new converts?

Pastor Boedeker: Any person brought to the Lord is followed up by the person who brought him. We use the Evangelism Explosion follow-up materials. We encourage new converts to begin in Discovery Class I, which studies the Navigators' Lessons in Assurance and begins the first Sunday of each month. Discovery II, which uses the Navigators' Lessons in Christian Living, is next. The third area of study involves a twenty-six-week introduction to the Old and New Testaments; we teach them to use their sword. So the new convert spends forty weeks in small group experiences with classes aimed at their specific needs. We also steer new converts to one of our growth groups, our home Bible studies, which require a two-year commitment. The growth group and the long-term home discipleship groups have been most instrumental in making Jesus real to our people.

Charles: What kind of discipling method do you use?

Pastor Boedeker: We use Churches Alive!, which recommends the Navigators' Design for

Discipleship study. Realize, though, that materials and programs can't produce disciples. People involved in the lives of people make disciples through the integral work of the Holy Spirit.

I also personally disciple three to five men one on one at any given time. I'm involved in my third group now. To be in that discipleship process, which takes about a year and a half, the men must commit to do the same thing with other men soon after our work together is over. We're into the second and third generation of that process, and now men are meeting with other men all over the place. Women do the same thing, although more in small groups than one on one.

Charles: Is the church involved in any specialized ministries?

Pastor Boedeker: People in this fellowship are burdened for prison ministries and give themselves there, but we don't organize that work. People sometimes fear some ministries because they're afraid they'll get in over their heads. For example, Dallas has a large homosexual community for whom we carry a burden. We consider them in bondage and as we've reached out, we've seen some miraculous transformations. We have a ministry to missionaries. About forty Wycliffe families make First Church their home church, and we offer them a place to rest and renew. Many of them return from intense spiritual warfare and need healing.

Our singles' ministry, our senior adult ministry, and other ministries have evolved as people have seen a need. A class for divorced people sprang up because the need was there. Hundreds and hundreds of dollars go out from this church to buy food and lodging for people who need help. We never turn away a legitimate need; some of the needy may be angels in disguise. Our community has thousands of needs. We have not studied all the needs and chosen some, although that can be helpful. Instead, we ask God to bring needs to our attention and then to raise up workers to meet that need.

Charles: Are there reasons other than program that First Church is successful?

Pastor Boedeker: We have an extremely strong male leadership base. Husbands accept their responsibility for spiritual leadership in their families. Husbands and wives team up in ministry. These couples provide invaluable role models for our young people. Two or three times a year, we offer resources for our families—marriage enrichment retreats, film series, seminars.

Another strength is expository preaching on the whole counsel of God. I pray about a need in our church and ask the Lord which book of the Bible might speak to the need. Then I preach through the book, not necessarily verse by verse, but at least topic by topic. Some of our people are gifted Bible scholars and teachers. Our church is based on the teaching of Scripture.

Charles: What is the mission of the First Church of God of Dallas?

Pastor Boedeker: We want to reach our community, our country, and the entire world. And that sounds trite. But we do it one person at a time, and we see every person as the next one ready for the Kingdom. When I came, our missions budget stood at fifteen hundred dollars for World Service. Now the missions budget is about forty thousand dollars, and I envision a day when a million dollars will go from this church into the world.

Charles: Can you share some of your goals as a church?

Pastor Boedeker: Our new facility is a short-term goal. The militantly evangelistic Bible studies I mentioned are a short-term goal. By the end of this year we want to begin an under-shepherd program so that every person in our fellowship will be shepherded by someone. Establishing the eldership as a governing board will require bylaw changes and a lot of other work; that's a short-term goal.

Long range . . . I believe God has given us a vision of what this church is to be. I talk about numbers, but every number is a changed life, and that's what excited me. At some point in the future, this church will minister to ten thousand people, including black and Hispanic congregations in this area. I believe we will be a discipling station for missionaries. All this will happen if our motives stay pure. If we're motivated by Jesus' vision of his ministry—to heal the brokenhearted, give sight to the blind, release the captives—our motives are pure. If our motivation is to compete with the church down the street, our ministry is over.

Charles: As you have grown, have you seen the growth through transfers or through first-time conversions?

Pastor Boedeker: The majority of our growth has come from transfers, people from other churches. We're not comfortable with the fact, but we do rejoice that these people have discovered the reality of Jesus through our ministry. These people are hungry for God, hungry for a place to grow and serve effectively. God has brought gifted, committed people to this church. While we reach for a larger percentage of growth from first-time conversions, we rejoice in the fruit of our ministry—taking in Christians and helping them be open and excited to the point that they're ready to be used.

Charles: What could other churches learn from this church? What concepts could transfer?

Pastor Boedeker: Jesus discipled a few men, asked them to count the cost, and poured his life into them until they shared his vision, his methods, and even his joy in the fruit of his ministry. That discipleship principle is the core of our work here. I think if we take the few that have a heart for God and pour our life and vision into them, the church will grow. The pastor has to have a vision, an understanding of the desire of God for the life of his congregation.

The small group effort is critical. People grow as they pray together, minister to one another's needs, and begin to pray about outreach. As the people grow, the church grows. Then as people mature in those groups, they need to be equipped to share their faith. For our church, that's the point of Evangelism Explosion. We want a teaching ministry that produces faith and vision.

Discussion

1. When Pastor Boedeker first came to Dallas, he found a problem that's common to many churches: lay people "had expected the pastor to do the things that . . . are their responsibility." He lists three of those things:

Witnessing _____

_____

_____

Developing Spiritual Gifts _____

_____

_____

Discipling Others _____

_____

_____

Review Ephesians 4. Then write beside each task the verse(s) that say lay people should be doing this rather than the pastor.

2. Pastor Boedeker says that "as the Holy Spirit leads us, we should be able to agree 100 percent on the decisions made by our leadership." Was this true in the New Testament church? (Give Scripture references to show.)

_____

_____

_____

Do you believe it can be true in today's church? Why or why not? _____

_____

_____

_____

3. Pastor Boedeker says that visitation shows people that we care, "but I don't think that's the way we'll win our community." Why doesn't he? _____

_____

_____

_____

What does he think is a *better* way to win his community? _____

_____

_____

_____

4. "God is our audience," Pastor Boedeker says. "People are performers. Those on the platform merely prompt." Let's see how this understanding of worship measures up against the Word. Read Psalm 66 and then explain what the Bible says are the worship functions of the following:

God (vs. 7, 19) _____

_____

_____

_____

the people (vs. 1-5, 13-17) _____

_____

_____

_____

the worship leaders (2 Chron. 23:12-13)_____

_____

_____

_____

Chapter 6

"We are ambassadors for
Christ in the nation's capital."

Chapter 6
Threshold, Household, and Vineyard
Pastor Samuel Hines

Overview

According to Pastor Sam Hines, Third Street Church of God serves a community of powerless people. The community has physically deteriorated since it was founded in the shadow of the United States Capitol building. Although a few families have lived in the area for many years, most of the people are poor and transient, depending upon absentee landlords who provide virtual shacks for housing. Drug traffic and some prostitution have invaded the area, but the real needs are for proper housing and employment.

The most pressing need is for role models. Most young people grow up in homes without fathers. Many more have fathers they cannot respect. Many women bear the burden of leading families and rearing children and are broken by the pressure. Many become alcoholics. Pastor Hines sees Third Street Church members as models for people in the community; the church leaders come from the area and can provide models for a better life while identifying with the area's needs.

Another urgent need is for help to negotiate the government systems that are supposed to aid people in the community. Third Street Church acts as a kind of broker for social services, directing people to offices that provide health care, Social Security counseling, job training, and other assistance. Without the help of the church, people are shuffled from one government office to another, spending food money for bus fare and burning with anger and frustration.

Third Street is seventy-one years old and is a stable congregation firmly committed to the Church of God movement. Brother and Sister Benjamin, pioneers from the West Indies, planted the congregation. Known as "Dad Benjamin," Brother Benjamin led the church for fifty-seven years. Many of the people in the congregation lived in the same building with the Benjamins, who maintained an open house for visitors from around the country.

The present building was completed in the 1940s. Pastor Hines lists expanded service and worship facilities as a high priority on the church's agenda. High real estate prices hinder this effort, but the work progresses. The morning worship attendance now averages three hundred persons.

The congregation at Third Street Church resists classification. Working side by side are the poor, people from the middle class, professional people, and government workers. The congregation has broken the racial barrier and seeks to continue its racial diversity.

Interview

Charles: Pastor Hines, what is the mission of Third Street Church of God?

Pastor Hines: I asked the Lord that when I came here thirteen years ago. The word I had from him has stuck in my mind all these years—*reconciliation.* It means preaching the gospel of reconciliation, pointing people to the mediator. Then also, it means building bridges between people so that fellowship and brotherhood replace alienation, isolation, separation, and all those other systems of the disease of sin. God's agenda is to bring all things to the Creator through Christ, and this is Third Street's agenda.

Charles: What is your leadership style?

Pastor Hines: I have a participatory charismatic leadership. I say *charismatic* because I believe the government of the Church is based on gifts of the Spirit—not on me or tradition, but on gifts of grace that God gives to enable ministry. I use the word *participatory* because I do not believe that the pastor has all the gifts. The entire community of believers must be inspired, enabled, nurtured, and discipled so that the whole body can effectively fulfull the ministry. I used to believe that ministry was built around the needs of the community. I have changed that belief. I'm now convinced that ministry is built around gifts, as in the New Testament times.

Charles: What is the main evangelistic strategy of the church now?

Pastor Hines: What excites me most is relational evangelism. In other words, we earn the right for direct evangelism by building relationships with people. The church has established a firm footing in the area because people see us as servants of the community, rather than exploiters of the community. I'm excited by the whole idea of sending people out to serve rather than to look for prospects. Of course, we do teach people how to share Christ in a personal way so that they can present the gospel clearly when a person opens the door.

However, I think all the church's life should be evangelistic. Our worship services are a combination of nurture and evangelism. Small groups meet to teach people how to share their faith. New believers come to a training class so that they can learn to witness while they are still young and fresh.

Charles: The congregation seems to find such joy in sharing the good news. How do you create a positive atmosphere for evangelism at Third Street?

Pastor Hines: When I first arrived, I began

doing two things. One was to identify the church, its nature, and its ministry. The second was to identify the world; where is the world, what is the world, and what is its relationship to the kingdom of God? Those two ideas led me into a lot of exegetical preaching to get a biblical base for understanding our mission. Then we implemented that understanding in several ways to make the church more conducive to evangelism.

First, we wrote a new church constitution and bylaws to make them more usable for evangelism and not just for administrative control. Then we established a style of church life based on five ministries: worship and fellowship, evangelism and missions, Christian education, music, and administration. We emphasized that all five are ministries and part of the church's general mission. We also developed a statement that identified the goal of this particular congregation. It begins, "We are ambassadors for Christ in the nation's capital." We refined that statement over several years and involved the whole congregation in the process. We see ourselves as a metropolitan church, not a community church or an inner-city church; we see all of greater Washington as our parish. This is an international city, and we have a sense of reaching the world, of being in the center of the action.

Charles: How many hours in the week are spent in purposeful direct evangelism?

Pastor Hines: I have a problem with that question; I have a problem with identifying slots of time for evangelism. For example, I know some churches have an evangelistic night when they go calling. We do not have such a night. Our feeling has been that we should motivate and train people to be on-the-job evangelists. Then they can come to church on Sunday and Wednesday to report and be renewed. We emphasize that our people should not come on Sunday just to see who is preaching but to introduce new people they have won for the Lord.

Charles: So you mean that people share Christ where they live in a life-style-type evangelism?

Pastor Hines: Life-style-type evangelism? Yes. But again we must always include very clear simple knowledge of the gospel so that our people can articulate the gospel when a door opens. Some people say to build relationships and then let the Lord do the evangelizing. I don't believe that's right. I believe the Lord wants us to carry through the process. That's why I keep repeating the gospel in training sessions and preaching events. I measure my preaching by whether people can make a crisp, clear statement of what the gospel is about. If they can't do that, they can't witness.

Charles: What about regular visitation among the church people?

Pastor Hines: General visitation is a high priority in our church. Most congregations believe that a pastor's work consists of preaching and visiting. No one pastor or two or three can adequately do the visiting. My visiting is selective. The associate pastor, the associate leaders, and I visit those in the hospital or sick at home. We visit the "squeaky wheel," those who call and ask for a visit. To visit everyone in the church, though, is impossible.

Charles: How are people encourged to visit one another?

Pastor Hines: The church has several fellowship groups, each one containing eight to ten families. Most of them are organized regionally. The leaders of these groups are responsible to make the group aware that they should visit each other and be accountable for each other. In some of the groups, the idea works well; in others, we are still working against the tradition that the pastor does all of the visiting.

Charles: What about visiting in the community outside the church?

Pastor Hines: We do a lot of visiting through One Ministries, which involves visiting the poor, sick, oppressed, and depressed people in the immediate community. That visitation is a must for us because those people need us most. The same people involved in that ministry also visit community leaders, the mayor, and congressmen. We make those leaders aware of the needs of the powerless people we serve.

Charles: Why are people attracted to Third Street Church? You have said that the building itself is sandwiched between rowhouses and people can pass by and not even see the church. What is the attraction?

Pastor Hines: They come because of relationships. We have been here seventy-one years building relationships. Some come through fraternal relationships. People come because of our leadership in the community. When you open yourself up to the community, when you're visible, people will track you down to your roots. And then we have a radio broadcast that brings people in. Some come from the West Indian and Jamaican communities because I am Jamaican. And some come for the preaching.

Charles: Let's talk a bit about new converts. Once the people come, how are they incorporated into the body?

Pastor Hines: When I first came here, I began the Threshold Class—threshold meaning "the door"—for new people. In the twelve weeks of the class I tried to present several important points: a portrait of the New Testament church; a portrait of the local church; an emphasis on assurance, to make sure these new people are anchored in the faith; and a study of stewardship, meaning responsibilities to God through the local church, through evangelism, and so forth. It is during the Threshold Class that people are first included in a fellowship group. New members can't know everybody, but in a fellowship group they can get to know those eight to ten families. The fellowship leaders are responsible to help the new members discover their gifts and how to build ministry around those gifts. Our job is to see that each person gets hooked into the body.

After the Threshold Class is the Household Class, which deals with the Spirit and the fruit of the Spirit. It explores the ethics, morals, and discipline of being a member of the Household of God.

The last class is the Vineyard Class. Each new member must become a worker in the Vineyard—sharing his faith and bringing the Harvest.

Charles: Part of what you have described is a discipling ministry. What specialized ministries is the church a part of?

Pastor Hines: For a long time we had a foster care program through which we placed delinquent and displaced children in group homes. We terminated that program because it involved us with bureaucrats more than with the children. We cannot provide day care because we don't have the facilities. Our One Ministries provides a strong community summer program; as many as two hundred children have participated. We get Christian young people, most of them college age, to supervise this summer program. These students, called deputies, are sponsored by their home churches. While they are here, we further disciple them and provide them with opportunities for Christian service. Another ministry that has impressive outreach is our work at Lawton Prison.

Charles: We have talked about community involvement, evangelism, and discipling leadership. What concepts at Third Street can transfer to other churches?

Pastor Hines: We must first remember that God loves the world. One of the biggest mistakes that the Church makes is to think that we are all God has and all God loves. We program that way and budget that way. The Church actually is just a little piece of the world that said "yes" to God. God is trying to show his love to the rest of the world, but he can only do that if the Church remembers she is watched by the world and behaves herself accordingly. The Church exists not for herself but for the world out there.

Second, I believe the Church must show the world that the Kingdom has come. There must be something in the Church that is beyond culture, nationality, race, class, education, and other such things. I believe the church falls down when she becomes too strongly tied to a particular culture. That is why I oppose the creation of white churches or black churches. There is nothing mysterious about a church made of people who look like each other and act like each other. But such a church says nothing very significant to the world, especially if the world feels unwelcome there. There must be something in the church that cannot be explained except by the fact that God lives in his people.

Third, I believe that we must look for allies. We do not believe that ghetto problems can be solved by ghetto people. The old cliche that a person can pull himself up by his bootstraps, that he can have a different life if he wants it, is blarney. Suburban people must be sensitized to the ghettos. We have found an ally here in the National Presbyterian Church. The pastor there is a brother in the Lord, in the Spirit. We have a kind of marriage between sensitive believers at National and sensitive believers at Third Street. I believe the Church must find allies, not calling them enemies because they are Presbyterians or whatever, but brothers because they are Christians.

Charles: Finally, how would you categorize Third Street Church? Is it a social-action church or a soul-winning church?

Pastor Hines: We need to coin a new word for the phenomenon at Third Street. I wouldn't ever want to be identified as a social-action church. You might say I want a church specializing in pity; but pity is not an end in itself. The only term that might apply is servant-model church. I like a church that's a servant model because it seems to fit what Jesus did when he was here.

Discussion

Jesus claims to be the way, the truth, and the life (John 14:6). He declares that he is the Son of God and the Savior of the world. This truth evokes a passion for evangelism in the heart of any true believer.

1. What are some other ways of life available to a person in Washington, D.C., besides the way of Jesus Christ? _____

_____

_____

_____

2. Pastor Hines says the Lord impressed him with the need for reconciliation. What is *reconciliation?* Base your answer on 2 Corinthians 5:18-21. _____

_____

_____

_____

3. Pastor Hines says, "My visiting is selective. . . . We visit those in the hospital or sick. We visit those who call and ask for a visit. To visit everyone in the church, though, is impossible." Is this policy true to the Bible standard? Study James 1:27 and 5:14 before you answer. _____

_____

_____

_____

4. Third Street Church has three levels of training for new converts—the Threshold Class, the Household Class, and the Vineyard Class. What special training does your church give to new converts?_____

_____

_____

_____

5. How might you strengthen your work in this area? _____

_____

6. Instead of building their ministry around community needs, the people of Third Street Church built their ministry around their own gifts. Is this approach true to the Bible? (Cite Scripture passages on which your answer is based.) _____

_____

_____

Chapter 7
A Church of Dreamers
Pastor Wayne Anderson

Overview

When builders complete Riverchase, four thousand families will live in this planned community ten miles south of Birmingham. Only six years old, the community already houses a few hundred families. Riverchase is an executive community with a white-collar life-style.

The pressure of an upwardly mobile life-style can strain family relationships. Climbing the success ladder often leaves dreams unrealized, and the church points to Jesus Christ as the ultimate fulfillment. Riverchase South responds to these needs and pressures in its community. As hearts and lives are left empty by executive success, the congregation is ready with the gospel.

Riverchase South grew out of a meeting of forty-seven people in June 1980. At that time, twenty people expressed interest in beginning a new church in the south Birmingham area. They immediately held Sunday evening services, and one month later added morning worship as well. Wednesday Bible studies met in homes. For nine months the congregation worked without pastoral leadership, although one person served in counseling and visitation. In March 1981, the Wayne Anderson family came to pastor the church, which at the time met in Hoover. Presently occupying temporary facilities at Valley Dale Terrace, the church has purchased ten acres in the Riverchase community. Excitement runs high as the church senses the need to expand its facilities and to establish a permanent home on the Riverchase property. The temporary facilities are inadequate, but area businesses and church people who live nearby open their buildings and homes for Sunday school.

In the first two years of Pastor Anderson's pastorate, attendance has grown from forty to ninety-five. Most of the congregation are young executive families. Some people are of retirement age; others are newlyweds. Considering the size of the congregation, the youth group is quite large—fifteen to twenty teen-agers attend Riverchase South.

Interview

Charles: Wayne, describe your style of leadership for me.

Pastor Anderson: I'm not a dictator, but I'm not a laissez-faire leader either. I try to take advantage of the gifts God has given this congregation. Some people here are better leaders than I am, and I am delighted to see them use their leadership gifts. We're well organized administratively. As a leader, I try to enable the lay people to do the work of ministry. I align myself with the pastor-teacher model of Ephesians 4.

Charles: You've seen a great deal of growth in a short time. How do you create a positive atmosphere for evangelism in this ministry?

Pastor Anderson: We might like to think we're creating a special atmosphere, but we're not. For the most part, our people simply realize what God is doing through them, and they tell their friends about it. Before I agreed to come here, I struggled to be sure I was responding to God's call and not just to the excitement in this church. These people are on fire for Jesus! When they invite others into their homes or talk with friends at work, their conversations center on the church and what God is doing here. Our people talk about the changes God has made in their lives. People in the community ask about the church, too. They might say, "I hear something exciting is happening down at Riverchase church. Tell me about it!" People just want to be a part of an exciting church where God is doing something.

So we haven't had to create an atmosphere

for evangelism; the excitement of our people just naturally leads to evangelism. To this point, I think our most effective means of evangelism has been that everyday kind of sharing as our people tell their friends about Christ.

Charles: There's an atmosphere of love and openness here that says you care about the community. In the worship service, two words ·jumped out at me: *love* and *give*. This is a very loving and giving group of people.

Pastor Anderson: And the third word is *vision*. One of our church slogans says "Welcome to our dream." Our people are dreamers. They really love others, and they're willing to sacrifice to demonstrate that love. They love people because they know God loves them. And they sacrifice because they see the vision of the church; they see where God is leading us. We talked earlier about the emptiness of corporate success, even at the top of the ladder. Some of our people reached all the way to that empty success, and now they've found real success in Jesus Christ. They want to share him with their colleagues who are pushing toward the same empty goal they achieved.

Charles: What is your evangelistic strategy?

Pastor Anderson: We're open to different strategies. We don't want to lock out something that might work just because we're locked into something else. As we wrestled to know our purpose as a church, we devised a statement: "We exist as a church to glorify God, and we do that through evangelism, through discipleship, and through outreach." To fulfill that purpose, we must be open to people and their needs.

We try as many different strategies as our gifts and talents allow. So we have an evangelism training program; we've mailed some brochures; we've run a newspaper ad; and we've invested time in the TV special "The Doctor Is In." People have responded to all those strategies. Our goal to this point has been to keep our church name in front of people, to establish ourselves as a caring congregation. We don't want to be just another church on just another corner. But in reaching our goals, our members' enthusiasm is our best approach.

Charles: Describe the evangelism training you offer.

Pastor Anderson: Fewer than a dozen people have taken that training in the year and a half we've offered it. Our people responded positively to a Wednesday night series I called "The Biblical Basis of Evangelism." We use several different approaches. Again, while first priority is sharing the gospel, the second and maybe more important priority is meeting needs so that people will *listen* to the gospel.

Charles: Is regular visitation a high priority?

Pastor Anderson: We don't have Sunday school visitation, but we continue with evangelism visitation. Sometimes we just knock on doors, introducing the church to the community. I take lay people with me when I make calls. I often make an appointment to talk with someone about getting involved in this type of evangelism. I don't press for an immediate response, but I do ask the person to pray and consider what God would ask of him.

Charles: Who are you trying to reach?

Pastor Anderson: We're not exclusive. We want to minister to all types of people. But we primarily target the Riverchase community, and that means white-collar, middle-class, white American executive families.

Charles: Why are people attracted to Riverchase South? If I were passing by, the building itself would not make me stop. What is the attraction?

Pastor Anderson: The excitement of our people. You're right about the building. It's not so enchanting it draws people off the street. But if we had the most attractive building in the world and no warmth, people wouldn't stay. They can't be attracted by a building very long. Most of the people who come do so because someone invites them or because they see something different in our people.

Charles: What do you do with new converts who come in?

Pastor Anderson: First, we want them to feel part of the family. Perfection is not a criterion for belonging here—nobody here is a finished product. We try to find a place for each person, something that fits his interests. If someone shows an interest in a particular committee, we don't make him wait three or four years to participate. Sometimes these new people present immature ideas because they don't understand the differences between the church and the world out there. We run the risk of their making some mistakes. We let them know that involvement here takes commitment, but we let them develop in their Christian commitment in their own way and time. We don't hold them at arm's length until they prove themselves. People are transformed at different rates. For some the change is immediate. For others, change progresses over weeks or months.

In practical terms, we give visitors a packet describing the ministries of the church. We have a newcomer's packet as well, and new people are invited to a newcomer's class.

Charles: How do you disciple people?

Pastor Anderson: We use several methods. We do not have a regular discipling class, but I ask a mature Christian to work one on one with every new Christian. I have chosen individuals to disciple myself. Our Sunday-school program offers discipleship classes, and some in-home groups involve discipling. We use as many methods as will work in this particular church.

Charles: Is the church involved in any specialized ministries such as jail ministry or ministry to the handicapped?

Pastor Anderson: Some of our people minister in nursing homes, and one person works in jail ministry. We've offered some neighborhood get-togethers with evangelism as the ultimate goals. I serve as hospital chaplain, and I approach it as a chance for evangelism. And we're cooperating with a day-care center in our area by offering a weekly Bible storytime.

Charles: Why is Riverchase South successful?

Pastor Anderson: It would be great if I could say the key is dynamic pastoral leadership! But honestly, that's not the reason. The love of our people makes this church successful. Our people are open. They'll try anything. Some people say it's easier for us to do that because our church has no traditions, but people bring tradition with them. And some of those traditions are good. We don't throw them out the windows just because they're traditions. Our people come from many different backgrounds and we enjoy many different traditions.

No, I would say this church is successful because we go out of our way to involve people, to help them feel part of us. Our lay leadership is dynamic. The church adapts its ministry to the needs of people. Someone shared with me that he has grown here, not because we say "yes, yes" together or "no, no" together, but because we say yes and no in harmony. People can be themselves and still be part of the fellowship. That freedom is one of our greatest assets.

Charles: What are your goals here?

Pastor Anderson: We want to establish a church building at a permanent location but not at the expense of our present ministry. We don't strive for numerical goals. We just seize the opportunities that are available. We place a high priority on evangelism; we talk it, we preach it, we sing it, and we live it. And we don't want our evangelism to stop with Riverchase. Through Faith Promise we provide half the support for our Hong Kong missionaries, Mike and Debbie Kinner. Some people from Tokyo lived with us for over a year. Now they're back in Tokyo and we try to touch that city through them.

Charles: What concepts have you developed that other churches might use in their ministries—especially smaller churches in situations similar to yours?

Pastor Anderson: First, if God opens a door to something, try it. That sounds big and scary, but if God provides an opportunity, he surely has the means to complete the work. Second, don't be afraid to be a little different from other churches. Third, let people know who and where you are. A church has to identify itself to the community. We've mailed our two brochures to this community, fourteen thousand pieces in all. It's expensive, but the exposure is worth the cost. And fourth, let people stretch themselves in the life of the church. Let them get involved. They will blossom.

Discussion

1. Pastor Anderson says, "I'm not a dictator, but I'm not a laissez-faire leader, either." (*Laissez-faire* is a French term, meaning, "Do as you please." A *laissez-faire* leader lets his followers do whatever they want.) Think about the biblical basis for this. Does the Bible say it's wrong for a pastor to be a dictator? for a pastor to be

a laissez-faire leader? (Cite Scripture passages to explain.)_____

_____

_____

_____

2. Pastor Anderson says that he tries to align with the pastor-teacher model in Ephesians 4. Read Ephesians 4:11-12 and describe in your own words what this scripture says a pastor should do. _____

_____

_____

_____

Is this all that the Bible says a pastor should do? (If not, list the other things the Bible puts in the pastor's job description—and give your references!)_____

_____

_____

_____

3. The people of Riverchase South have a lot of excitement about Jesus. But did you hear anything in the interview to indicate that they're getting grounded in the Word of God, too? (Any other words, any clues that they're developing a *mind* for Christ as well as a *heart* for him?) _____

_____

_____

_____

4. How exciting is it to read about people who *ask* about what is happening in a church! Maybe that doesn't happen to you very often. But it was very common in New Testament times. Read John 12:20-21. Why did these Greeks (Gentiles) ask to see Jesus? (Check the preceding verses.)_____

_____

_____

_____

Bible scholars believe these Greeks asked Philip because he was a Gentile, too. (He was from Bethsaida, a predominantly Gentile city.) What sort of people are most likely to ask *you* about Jesus?_____

_____

_____

_____

What should you do when someone asks you about Jesus—or about what Jesus is doing in your congregation? (Consider what Philip did, verse 22.) _____

_____

5. Take a closer look at the four things Pastor Anderson said your church could learn from their experience. List specific things your church could do along these lines:

Insight   *What My Church Could Do*

1. If God opens a
   door to something,
   try it.

2. Don't be afraid to
   be a little different
   from other
   churches.

3. Let people know
   who you are and
   where you are.

4. Let people stretch
   themselves in the
   life of the church.

Chapter 8

Chapter 8

Everything Has a
Hook in It

Pastor David Grubbs
Pastor Don Taylor
Pastor Greg Wiens

Overview

Dayton is a move-out community. In the
last fifteen years the city has lost thirty-
five thousand jobs. In 1968, National Cash
Register employed twenty-one thousand people;
today the payroll is four thousand. Frigidaire
has eliminated eight thousand jobs and Dayton
Tire and Rubber three thousand. Six thousand
automotive workers are unemployed. A mid-
western city built by traditional industry, Dayton is caught between that tradition and the
new technological age.

Yet the city appears now to have stabilized.

While the city has lost 40 percent of its population in the last fifteen years, most of these people have simply moved to Dayton's suburbs. Innovations in technology invite new industries to replace the city's outdated factories. Wright Patterson Air Force Base invigorates the economy by offering forty thousand jobs, most of them civilian.

Dayton needs jobs and a larger industrial tax base to support the schools, but beyond that Dayton needs a new spirit, what Pastor David Grubbs calls the spirit of hope and optimism. By building a stunning $4.5-million facility and continuing to grow, Salem Church has encouraged pride and hope in northwest Dayton. The community has caught the church's optimism. Northwest Dayton is not a glamorous growth area, but the church decided to build there because Interstate 70 makes it accessible from all directions.

In addition to jobs and a renewed spirit, the people of Dayton need help with their families. Salem Church shoulders its responsibility to counsel and teach God's view of marriage and family relationships.

Sociologically, Salem violates every rule of the church growth movement. On any given Sunday, about 70 percent of the congregation are middle class and about 20 percent are lower class. Most of the congregation are well-employed, but not wealthy, high school and college graduates. The church had not sought to attract wealthy people at first, fearing the newcomers would reject the church or introduce liberal thinking, but this attitude has changed. In the last decade, wealthy, highly cultured, executive families have come to make up about 10 percent of the congregation. About fifty people represent minorities at Salem Church, and the largest groups of people are Southerners and Appalachians. A Korean family, a Mexican family, and families from Vietnam also make Salem their church home.

Salem Church began in 1895 as a cottage prayer meeting. Itinerant evangelists boosted the church by holding tent meetings three or four times a year. From the time the congregation occupied its first building in 1913 to the mid-1930s the church steadily progressed. In the early 1940s, attendance peaked at four hundred. After that time a series of moves to smaller facilities chipped away at the church; in 1968, average attendance was 217. When Pastor Grubbs preached his first Sunday evening service, forty-three people came.

In the fifteen years of Pastor Grubbs' work here, the church has steadily advanced. Average attendance now is about fifteen hundred. Double worship services began in mid-1983.

Interview

Charles: Has your leadership style changed over the past fifteen years?

Pastor Grubbs: Sure. My intentions are the same, but growth and necessity force me to change. Without change a pastor stagnates or moves every few years. Before our staff had to grow, I could be a free-wheeling pastor, a Lone

Ranger. Now I'm a manager. I'm responsible for and accountable to twenty employees. I'm not entirely comfortable as a manager, but it's a necessary part of growing. Any man who leads a growing church will learn to adapt his leadership style and life-style, or he will die. On the other hand, he may reach a certain level and say, "There. That's all the people I want to be bothered with." That's not necessarily wrong. But I wanted to stretch my potential to its capacity before I did.

Charles: How do you create a positive atmosphere for evangelism?

Pastor Grubbs: First of all, I believe in it. I demonstrate evangelism by my preaching, lifestyle, example in leadership, and carefully structured instruction. It all begins with the senior pastor. I know of no church that has hired a staff person to set the church on a course of evangelism without the direct involvement of the senior pastor. The senior pastor may become less involved administratively in the evangelistic work of the church. But unless his heart is evangelistic, unless his preaching, teaching, and day-to-day walk demonstrate evangelism, the church will not be evangelistic.

Charles: And you encourage your staff to do likewise?

Pastor Grubbs: I do more than encourage. I require. Anyone who doesn't reproduce other Christians is an ex-employee, because we can't teach people to be evangelistic if the paid leaders are not.

Charles: What is the basic evangelistic strategy of this church?

Pastor Grubbs: There are several. The most obvious strategy is the pulpit. People do respond to persuasive, biblical preaching. Every week since we moved into this new building in 1981, people have come forward to make first-time decisions for Christ. These are not decisions made during the week and later affirmed at the altar, but decisions made in response to the preaching. Trained counselors meet people at the altar and later follow up on them.

Charles: Has response to the altar changed in the last year or two?

Pastor Grubbs: It's increasing as far as people coming to pray for salvation. Even the shape of the building makes coming to the altar easy. We now have eight aisles on the main floor and two from the balcony. The sloped floor helps people get started. The building doesn't make anyone come, of course, but when the atmosphere is conducive to making decisions, people find it easier to respond.

We don't apologize for the altar. The altar is not a point of browbeating at all. The altar is an attractive and enjoyable place. We trained and certified sixty altar counselors, and they're working at the altar before you know it. They get right to the point.

Charles: What about other evangelism strategies?

Pastor Taylor: Our basic training is the Evangelism Explosion (E.E.) program. It's been our raw material for evangelism for thirteen years. Pastor Grubbs started by taking sixty-six people to a Campus Crusade Here's Life Institute to learn to use the Four Spiritual Laws. Then he went to Coral Ridge in Florida to receive training in the E.E. program. With minor adjustments, E.E. can be implemented in almost any church. You don't need a full-time minister of evangelism to use it because the program is already developed.

Pastor Grubbs: Besides E.E., we offer weekend training which starts with a seminar on Friday night. For three hours then and for three hours on Saturday morning, the people learn and practice witnessing to each other. In the afternoon we send them out to downtown streets, shopping centers, and residential areas. We see decisions, but the retention rate is not high. We don't consider them conversions until they are aligned with the body of Christ and in nurture.

Another strategy is home Bible studies. At certain times people bring their friends to these home meetings to hear the gospel presented. We also teach people in discipleship groups to share their faith. And people are won through retreats, especially youth and singles. We also present special events such as musicals and concerts. These events draw a lot of the secular world and we make a clear-cut invitation to Christ. People respond to the invitation.

Charles: Explain more about your use of Evangelism Explosion. How many people are involved?

Pastor Taylor: In the last fifteen-week training class, twenty trainers had two trainees each— sixty people. Other people are involved as prayer partners. Overall, E.E. touches about two hundred people each semester through prayer partner relationships.

Charles: How many hours do you and those sixty people spend in purposeful evangelism?

Pastor Taylor: At that point, I'd have to define evangelism. Our classes meet on Thursdays, but that's the night for training, not for evangelism. In other words, we want to train for a life-style, not a once-a-week effort. Every week we ask the class to write down the evangelistic activities they were involved in that week. This helps them see that they can't wait until Thursday. Thursday is only the training ground. In terms of structured time, we expect people to study four to five hours a week, including Scripture memorization. Add class time and each person has to commit eight or nine hours a week to be effective.

Pastor Grubbs: God uses a million methods— preaching evangelism, writing evangelism, counseling evangelism, house-to-house evangelism. But the staff spends no less than 10 percent and maybe 20 percent of our time intentionally searching for new people. Figuring the number of hours is hard because everything we do is related to our clear statement of purpose: "To glorify God through provoking spiritual maturity among our people, so that beginning in our own home and reaching out to the ends of the earth, we seek to introduce people to Christ, help them to grow up in Christ, and teach them how to multiply in Christ." It's very simple, and yet it's hard because it goes against the tide of typical Christianity.

Charles: Is regular visitation a high priority here?

Pastor Grubbs: Oh, yes. We are swamped with visitors to our services. We do some door-to-door visitation, but we're at our limit just visiting prospects and people in the hospitals.

Pastor Taylor: Our women's group visits forty people a month in hospitals and another forty who are shut-in. We do other kinds of visitation, but evangelism visitation is critical. We want our people to see that while the church is attractive and fellowship is warm, evangelism is what we're all about.

Charles: How do you recruit people for evangelism training and visitation?

Pastor Grubbs: In Evangelism Explosion the trainers personally recruit their trainees. Not everyone should be involved in that program, so we do not usually recruit from the pulpit. We do recruit at large for the weekend crash-course evangelism classes.

Pastor Taylor: When an E.E. trainer looks for trainees, he visits them, leaves a book called *Fishers of Men,* and promises to return in a week to discuss the potential trainees' involvement. We don't ask whether God wants them involved, but rather *how* he wants them involved. If we're starting a new semester and we don't have enough trainees, we'll announce the program to the congregation at large, but we prefer to contact people personally and give them details of the program one to one. We want them to be sure of their commitment to the program. E.E. is a heavy course, and we don't want to surprise anyone.

Twice a semester, our evangelism teams just knock on doors or talk to people in laundromats and shopping malls. They use a questionnaire to screen people, to gauge their interest in hearing about Christ. Usually we call on visitors or others with whom we've had some contact, but for those two nights each semester, the teams just knock on doors. We don't see a lot of long-term fruit from this approach, but it stretches the trainers and trainees. They're afraid to go, but going teaches them that God is faithful and that people hunger for us to overcome our fear and share the gospel.

Charles: What kind of people are you trying to reach?

Pastor Grubbs: All kinds. Anybody. Peers reach peers, so we're going to bring in the kind of people we already have. As an example, one man got converted in the state penitentiary and came here because his sister comes here. Now he's bringing other ex-convicts because he understands them and they understand him. Like duplicates like. A church consists of many homogeneous groups. If six or eight people of one type buddy together, they can survive even though there aren't two hundred more just like them. In twenty-eight years of ministry, I've learned that a dozen people racially, culturally, intellectually, or economically alike will reproduce themselves within the Body.

Charles: How are people attracted to this congregation?

Pastor Taylor: People generally are attracted by the people who are here. Dave's preaching is evangelistic, and people know if they bring their friends they're going to have a chance to make a decision. And they know we'll visit their friends, too.

Pastor Grubbs: I'd agree that most people are attracted through personal recommendations of satisfied people. And we try to be the center of the evangelical experience in greater Dayton. In music, in outstanding speakers, in films, in marriage enrichment, we want to be good in Dayton. People come to those special events. Then people are very tenderhearted at Easter and Christmas, and they come in droves. We get their names and visit them. Summertime and the dead of winter are good times for youth work. Singles seminars bring people, too.

Pastor Wiens: And the facility attracts people. I've met people who came because they wanted to see what kind of church builds this kind of building. The preaching, the music, the alive worship all bring people in. They hear something pertinent to their lives.

Charles: When new people come and they make a decision for Christ, what do you do with them?

Pastor Grubbs: We begin in the home or at the altar—wherever the decision is made. We're careful to record the name, address, phone number, and a description of what the counselor thinks has happened. Then the discipleship and follow-up minister assigns a follow-up supervisor to the new Christian. The supervisor is responsible to make four calls and to get the new person into the new Christian's class. The class runs twenty-six weeks and is taught by two people who were won through the evangelism program. They're convinced of the need for assurance, Bible knowledge, and prayer. We also try to get new people into a neighborhood fellowship group, and some new people get involved in choir, women's ministries, and other groups.

Pastor Wiens: When I first came here, I talked with Christians who were reproducing themselves and asked, "How do you grow?" Invariably a pastor or layperson had taken them under his wing. But we had no organized effort. Beyond the E.E. materials, follow-up was minimal. Only a small percentage of new believers took the Christian Basics class. With the church's emphasis on evangelism, people were coming, but the quality of their growth depended almost solely on the pulpit. I don't discount the pulpit, but a person can't be fed adequately by preaching alone.

My vision for the church is to develop a comprehensive follow-up through discipling. To me that means teaching a person from his spiritual birth until he can reproduce Christ in others—not just win others, but disciple them as well. All parts of the ministry work together in discipleship. For example, Sunday school teacher training demands more than a five-week class on how to teach. Training teachers means bringing them to a level of spiritual maturity on a daily basis.

We use several discipleship methods. Some groups use *Design for Discipleship,* some use *Churches Alive!* and others use the *2:7 Series.* I also meet one on one with those I'm discipling myself. I meet with them at regular times every week.

Charles: Are you reproducing yourself spiritually?

Pastor Wiens: Yes, and that's scary. First, a person has to be discipled before he can disciple someone else, and while Paul said "Follow me as I follow Christ," I have not followed Christ perfectly. The people I'm discipling have seen me in situations in which I've had to say with humility, "I've blown it." It is good for people to realize that I'm not on a pedestal. Discipling has to be brother to brother; there has to be trust and honesty that allow me to confess to God and my brother that I'm maturing, too. The only way to build that trust and honesty is to let people live with me and see all my imperfections. It's scary.

My goal in the church is to provide opportunities for people to be discipled. Some people are not willing to go beyond a certain level of spiritual growth. I recognize that and have designed our discipleship program on three levels: one, the basic level of welcoming people into the body and incorporating them into a neighborhood group which meets once a month for Christ-centered fellowship; two, the once-a-week discipling groups; and three, discipling one to one.

Charles: What other forms of outreach do you use? Any specialized ministries?

Pastor Grubbs: We don't have a specialized jail ministry or a coordinated work with alcoholics. The singles ministry is highly specialized. And three or four times a year our youth get into the high schools with a special speaker on alternatives to drugs or strengthening the family or another topic. The kids listen and then our youth tell them about another meeting later that night—scores of kids have come this way. Mike Kersh, our minister of youth, trains the kids to be aggressive on campus, to share their faith. In another outreach, two of our men have organized a Bible study at the Holiday Inn north of town. Eight out of ten of the people who come never darken our church door, but they're nurtured by these two men who got their vision from this church and who are trained in evangelism. Another group of lay people take video tapes of our morning services to nursing homes. Those lay people are trained in evangelism, too. Then before last Easter, we printed twenty thousand brochures about our church. We divided our region by zip codes and distributed those brochures in four days. More than three thousand people came to church that Easter to see *Resurrection*.

Charles: So you use music ministry as an outreach?

Pastor Grubbs: Everything we do is motivated. If we advertise something or do something, you can bet your boots we've got a hook in it.

Charles: Other than the programs we've discussed, why is this church successful?

Pastor Grubbs: First, the staff and key leaders have accepted the vision of the senior pastor. I don't say this in arrogance, but I have a clear idea of where I'm going and how to get there. We understand our first priority.

Second, the spontaneous joy that comes out of our worship is terrific. The singing is delightful, and the preaching is intelligent and biblical. No church grows very long unless there's joy in worship.

Charles: What lessons have you learned at Salem Church that other churches could adapt?

Pastor Grubbs: Start small, grow slowly, and be patient. Don't get in a hurry to grow. Growth is a by-product, not an objective. We never have set numerical goals—four hundred or three thousand on a given Sunday. Such goals are counterproductive. If you miss the goal, people are depressed. But if you reach the goal, you take the focus off the mission of the Church, which is to reach people with the claims of Christ and help them grow to maturity. It's impossible to get spiritual maturity with gimmicks. We're reaching for spiritual maturity with New Testament principles and good management. So we believe that if the objectives are worthwhile and biblical, growth will come. But you have to start with a small tree and faithfully cultivate it. You can't dig up mature trees from someone else's woods and stick them in your yard. Transplanted programs, transplanted ideas, even transplanted leaders are rarely as effective as homegrown ones that have been patiently cultivated.

I also believe that a pastor must plan to give a church a significant part of his life if he wants it to grow. I don't believe in short-term pastorates. If I couldn't invest ten years of my life in a church, I wouldn't invest one.

Let me just say we're an ordinary church. We are a balanced church. We stress quality worship that has both excitement and content. I work hard at biblical preaching that's delivered with persuasion and conviction. We work hard to cultivate lay leaders and their gifts to be used in the body of Christ. We don't do anything unusual. We just do a lot of things persistently and faithfully.

Editor's Note: After serving fifteen years as pastor of Salem Church Pastor Grubbs resigned to accept a full-time position as an evangelist with the Board of Mass Communications.

Discussion

1. Christians have a duty to keep the Good News alive through each generation. As we share Christ's love from grateful hearts, we

insure the perpetuation of the Christian faith. This is what Pastor Grubbs meant about "reproducing" other Christians. Once you've led someone to Christ, what else should you do to make sure you've spiritually reproduced yourself in that person's life? (See 2 Timothy 2:1-2 and 2 Corinthians 2:14-16.) _____

_____

_____

_____

2. Pastor Grubbs says every worship service brings people to the altar and many of them to get saved. How would you assess your church's altar response? _____

_____

_____

_____

Should you do anything to encourage more people to come to the altar? _____

_____

_____

_____

3. Home Bible studies are also important at Salem Church. Think back to the beginning of your congregation; did the first people of your church have home Bible studies? (You might talk with some of your pioneers or consult your church scrapbook, if you can't remember.) ____

Are home Bible studies as vital to your work now as they were then? _____

_____

_____

_____

4. Pastor Grubbs says, "We want to be good in Dayton." What does he mean by that? _____

_____

_____

_____

How "good" is your church in your community? _____

_____

_____

_____

5. Pastor Wiens leads a discipling ministry at Salem Church. Describe in your own words what he's doing. _____

_____

_____

_____

Who might lead such a discipling ministry in your congregation? _____

_____

_____

_____

6. "If we advertise something or do something," Pastor Grubbs says, "you can bet your boots we've got a hook in it." What sort of "hook" does he mean?_____

_____

_____

_____

Do you agree that every church activity should have this "hook?" Why?_____

_____

_____

_____

Review your church calendar for this month. Does every activity have this "hook" in it? _____

_____

_____

_____

Chapter 9

"We don't make any money
on our day-care center but
we are reaching children and
their families."

Chapter 9

We Must Be Accessible
Pastor Farrell Berry

Overview

San Diego sprawls along the southern California coast and is home to eight hundred thousand people. The Clairemont Church of God serves a suburban area just north of San Diego proper. The 150,000 people who live in Clairemont are primarily middle-class whites, although Orientals and Hispanics are well represented. Clairemont is about twenty-five years old, a full-grown community. Some condominiums and apartment complexes are going up in Clairemont, but most new building is scheduled north and east of the suburb.

The Clairemont Church of God is people from all walks of life. One family is from Japan; another is Puerto Rican. Many people have retired. Many are single or divorced. The church generally reaches white, middle-class, white- and blue-collar workers. The majority of the congregation have no Church of God background at all.

The Clairemont church finished its new building in 1979. The sanctuary already is crowded, although space for Sunday school and children's church will be adequate for some time.

When asked about the needs of San Diego and Clairemont, Pastor Berry first said, "Reaching people with the gospel of Christ." California provides numerous social services, but the church alone offers spiritual help. The Clairemont church runs a day-care center motivated by the opportunity to show children the love of Christ. This concern for children drives a large part of Clairemont's ministry.

Interview

Charles: Where is this church going? What's your purpose for being here?

Pastor Berry: Our number one concern is meeting the needs of this community, reaching people for Christ. We do have long-range plans for buildings, but not just for the sake of building something. If we could meet all of the needs in the parking lot, we'd do it. We strive to meet people for the Lord, to bring them into the fellowship and help them grow.

We want to reach people for Christ. That's our only purpose, our only goal. We could set a numerical goal. We could say, "Let's reach three hundred or four hundred. That's a respectable number." But then we see one more boy or one more girl who needs Christ. So we can't limit our ministry.

Think about our day-care center. We don't make any money on it, not even enough to pay the utility bill. But even if it never earns a dime, we want to share love with these little kids. We want to sit them in a circle and teach them about Jesus Christ. Our Christian teachers and helpers show these children that we love them without a doubt. If it weren't for that chance to show love, we'd shut down the day care. But we are reaching children and their families. Each precious little child knows that God loves him, and we love him.

Charles: Tell me about the leadership style you bring to your people.

Pastor Berry: I'm a pastor. I love people. But love needs organization and training. My staff makes a big difference. I guide them and train them, but we accomplish a lot because each staff person does his job. It's a team concept. We're excited about working together.

I am concerned not only about pastoral leadership but also about lay leadership. We're aggressive leaders. We do our best to lead people to an end, but at the same time we try to be tender and humble. Whether we're painting buses or training for evangelism, we work right with our people. When we train leaders, we magnify the task so that people will see their jobs as vital to the church and to the Lord. Even if the job is changing the oil on the buses, we help people see that the work is for the Lord.

Charles: How do you create a positive atmosphere for evangelism?

Pastor Berry: First, the leadership is positive. If the pastor is positive, the people are positive. It's the only attitude our people ever see. We get our people involved in the work of the church. If they only sit in Sunday school and morning worship, there's no challenge. They'd probably backslide without a challenge.

At a recent Christian education conference we emphasized this positive enthusiasm. We want our teachers to understand the blessing that comes from serving the church. We encourage our people to find that blessing. For example, if we need a Sunday school teacher, we don't act desperate for a teacher. We choose a person and say to him, "We are concerned about finding a place for you in the church that meets your spiritual grace, your abilities. We feel this position is where God wants you to serve." We talk with people one to one. The response is wonderful.

Charles: What overall evangelistic strategy do you have? What is the overarching purpose of your evangelistic thrust?

Pastor Berry: We are deeply concerned about doing what the Lord commands. I think an empty church dishonors God. We follow the command of Jesus to go into the highways and compel people to come in. We use many methods of evangelism, but we're driven by our burden for people. Doing the Lord's work halfway, dishonors him.

Charles: Do you train your people in personal evangelism?

Pastor Berry: We have ten-week sessions each year. We're not trying to get everyone involved in lay witness training, but we do want to be effective. We want the witnesses to learn to share the gospel so that sharing becomes their way of life. In the last two sessions we trained five teams. A Methodist church brought three teams to our last session. We don't spend a lot of time in the classroom. The teams meet for twenty or thirty minutes, visit people with whom we've made appointments, and then return to the church to share results. We've had a problem finding enough prospects to keep the witnesses effective and excited. There has to be a challenge; just visiting is not enough. The witnesses have to apply themselves, to believe they are achieving something. During the ten weeks of training we don't see many commitments or decisions for Christ. Besides the people who are saved, the major benefit is the strengthening of the witness. To people who have been Christians for a long time, the lay-witness training is like hearing the gospel for the first time. We speak so much in cliche's that getting back to the basics of salvation really makes the gospel fresh again. We try to get new converts involved in lay witness because they're still on fire and the training helps ground them. The training gives them a solid base and helps them express their new faith.

Another advantage of the lay-witness training is its ability to get people outside themselves. A group of our young adults wanted to be in Bible study every night, but then they only satisfied themselves. Involving them in lay witness helps them share with others, not just please themselves.

Charles: How many hours (in any given week) does the church spend in purposeful evangelism?

Pastor Berry: Our bus captains meet on Saturday mornings for training and then visit for two to four hours. Sundays involve two to four more hours of bus work. That's about fifty-four hours a week, not counting any counseling time.

Charles: Tell me more about the bus ministry.

Pastor Berry: We run six routes, one of them in a mobile home area for senior citizens. We send buses to Mirror Mesa, a white collar area. One bus goes to Linda Vista, which is people connected with the navy. We don't go into any real slum areas. The buses make us visible in the community—they're red, white, and blue. Even if they didn't pick up a soul, those buses effectively advertise the church. They're the best billboard we have. We want to reach children and their parents. If the bus ministry becomes obsolete, if it ceases to meet needs, we'll drop it.

Charles: What kind of people are you trying to reach?

Pastor Berry: We are trying to reach any person who is sensitive to Christ. Our church is open to any kind of person. We reach a hand of love to anyone, whether he is shabbily or finely dressed. We're concerned about children. At the same time, we care about teen-agers, young adults, singles, senior citizens. We don't set out to reach a certain class.

Charles: There's a feeling in this church that something is happening. Why are people attracted to this church?

Pastor Berry: I think the main attraction is person-to-person contact. Nobody comes to hear a charismatic leader or an outstanding preacher. Our advertising is minimal. But we have a tremendous spirit of love and a spirit of growth. This is a live church. The word gets out through personal contact. One man heard about us over the CB radio and now this is his church home.

Charles: What part of your ministry brings in the most converts?

Pastor Berry: We don't overdo or underdo in any area. Conversions come from lay witness, bus ministry, worship services—all areas of ministry. I counsel many people, and we see conversions from that involvement. We have good response to the altar in our services.

Charles: How are new converts assimilated into the life of the church?

Pastor Berry: If an established Christian comes, we sit down with him and determine what gifts and interests he brings with him. We recommend a class and try to plug him into the work, because a working Christian is a happy Christian. We believe our job as pastors is to train our people to be involved in the ministry.

For new converts, we follow up with lay-witness materials. We encourage the new Christian to take our basic Christian doctrine class. We're weak on social activities, but just working together in the church satisfies that social need. If people want a social group, they can find them right and left in San Diego. We offer help in the spiritual realm.

Charles: How do you disciple new converts?

Pastor Berry: I do one-on-one Bible study with some of the men of the church. Sometimes I take them with me when I visit. The discipleship ministry needs to be developed; we're weak in that area. We also need a plan for leadership development.

I've been here ten years and we've come a long way, but we've had to build the program. We have emphasized outreach. Now it's time to develop other areas in which we are delinquent.

Right now we're phasing in our new youth pastor. I'll be released from the youth responsibilities and can give more time to leadership development and discipleship.

Charles: Do you have specialized ministries? Jail ministry, bar ministry, anything like that?

Pastor Berry: We don't have anything like that. We are developing a ministry to young adults, young people out of high school. And we're working with young couples, too. Right now those ministries are in the embryo stage.

Charles: Are there reasons other than the program that this church is successful?

Pastor Berry: God's blessing.

More important than the program is concern for the needs of people. We only have a program so we can meet those needs. We look at our community, and we live here with our people; we try to meet their needs. If the program ever stops meeting needs, we'll junk it and look for another.

Charles: What other things are bringing about success?

Pastor Berry: The love people find at Clairemont. And we are not a critical church. A person can come from a charismatic background, for instance, and we have strong communication with him.

We make our guidelines very clear; he can work, function, and be himself in our fellowship without promoting charismatic doctrine. Southern California people have more diverse backgrounds than you can shake a stick at. The church can't be dogmatic or denominational. We still preach and teach what the Bible teaches. We are still strongly Church of God. But the church must be accessible to those with different backgrounds. We are Christ-centered, and we emphasize the unity of believers. We don't spend a lot of time on peripheral issues.

Charles: So you are open and flexible, building a level of trust. What lessons could be learned from your ministry? What concepts developed here might transfer to other congregations?

Pastor Berry: Much of what happens here comes from the leadership, and I don't mean that as a brag. The pastoral staff has to be aggressive.

The pastor can't be dictator; he has to earn his right to lead. He has to be loving, but he also has to know where he's going and how he's going to get there. This is not bragging. I am humbled even to think that what has happened is just God. The key to growth is spiritual leadership within the church—balanced, aggressive, loving leadership. A church can only go as far as its leaders can go. So I think our leaders must be open and concerned about improving themselves. I include myself in that. We don't have all the answers. We need to expand ourselves and open ourselves to the leading of the Holy Spirit.

Charles: If you were to classify this church, how would you do it? Is it a soul-winning church? A social-action church? A teaching church?

Pastor Berry: Again, we strive for balance. We want to win souls, but we want to teach and nurture as well. We are not a social-action church. We're a loving church, a loving fellowship. And we put the Bible in the center of all we do.

Discussion

1. "We get our people involved in the work of the church," Pastor Berry says. "They'd probably backslide without a challenge." Do you agree? Why or why not?_____

_____

_____

_____

2. Not many people are won to Christ through Clairemont's lay-witness training. What other benefits make up for that? _____

_____

_____

_____

3. Notice what Pastor Berry says Clairemont is *not* doing: "Our advertising is minimal. . . . We're weak on social activities. . . . The discipleship ministry needs to be developed; we're weak in that area." Yet, the church is growing. Why? _____

_____

_____

_____

4. "The key to growth is spiritual leadership within the church. . . . A church can go only as far as its leaders can go." Do you agree? _____

_____

_____

_____

What should be some qualities of a church leader? _____

_____

_____

_____

5. Pastor Berry concludes that they "put the Bible at the center of all [they] do." Review Acts 2:4 and note how Scripture influenced the life of the New Testament church._____

_____

_____

_____

Chapter 10

"The church must use its
gifts where the world is.
That's why we go to the
marketplace."

Chapter 10
Make a Difference in People's Lives
Pastor Gilbert Davila

Overview

Iglesia de Dios in Corpus Christi serves a lower income Hispanic *barrio,* or neighborhood, on the west side of the city. The community neither grows nor shrinks; although some persons reared in the *barrio* leave for school or jobs, family ties often draw them back.

From Pastor Davila's point of view, the community needs the gospel above all. Iglesia de Dios changes its neighborhood. When the congregation built its facilities, the Oklahoma Bar stood right across the street. The church grew, eventually rented the land under the bar, and then removed that influence from the *barrio.* Several similar establishments in the area have been closed through the witness of the church.

The church works hand in hand with federal and state programs designed to help the community, offering social help such as Head Start as well as spiritual help. The church itself has become a sort of institution in the bario. But most of its influence is seen in lives changed by the gospel. The Word enhances lives roughened by *barrio* life.

In the late 1950s, a young minister from the West Coast started Iglesia de Dios as a home meeting. A second young pastor, whose pastorate spanned thirteen years, led the church to erect its first building. Several remodelings have brought the building to its present location. The church needs more sanctuary space, more classrooms, and more parking. As frustrated as the congregation is by the cramped conditions, they understand the need to preach the Word, to do the best they can with what they have.

In the eleven years of Gilbert Davila's pastorate, the congregation's profile has shifted from lower class economically to lower, lower-middle, and middle class. Many of the congregation are second- and third-generation attenders. Although services used to be entirely in Spanish, the church is now bilingual. The morning worship attendance now averages over two hundred.

Interview

Charles: What is the mission of this congregation, Pastor Davila?

Pastor Davila: The longer one serves the Lord,

the more clearly one sees. Our mission is not the number of people we bring in. In fact, numbers don't excite us any more. Our mission is to do the will of God as the Church, as a body of believers. We believe that we are not merely to exist on this corner as just another church, but we are here because God called us to this particular place. For a time we debated every new ministry we started. Should we? Shouldn't we? Now our vision is clearer, and our people are ready to do whatever God calls us to do.

The Book of Isaiah says to preach the Word and set captives free. In John 11, Jesus tells Lazarus to come forth, and he tells his disciples to loosen him. That's what God is telling us: Preach the Word to the community. Make a difference around the community and in the lives of people. And we have seen results even in the lives of our own leaders. They are effective witnesses because many people knew them before they were saved. People know what their lives used to be. Now people can see God at work in the lives and families of these leaders.

Charles: What is your leadership style as pastor?

Pastor Davila: That's a difficult question. I do love my people, and I let them know it. I encourage my people to take training. In our Hispanic background is a tendency to think we don't need training because we have done this work all of our lives. So I strongly encourage discipleship and training. People seeking positions or ministries within the church know they have to prepare themselves. And we don't just encourage preparation; we also make some of that training available.

I have been to discipleship clinics and read books, and I've discovered there is no one way to do anything. You have to do what works best where you are. Training reaches a point at which people need to be themselves. My people aren't systematic. They express themselves and learn orally. They're doers.

My leadership involves guiding the process, but sometimes I have to say, "I'm the pastor; let's do this or not do this. Let's stick to basics. Let's go with what we are doing."

Charles: Do you see yourself as the pastor/teacher?

Pastor Davila: Very much so. I also know I am a young pastor and that some of my people are schooled in Christian education. I used them to teach others. But I am the basic teacher.

Charles: How do you create a positive atmosphere for evangelism?

Pastor Davila: My wife and a couple of women from the congregation designed banners for the sanctuary that help set the climate for evangelism. One banner reads, "Go into all the world and preach the gospel." Another one reads, "You will receive power and you will be my witnesses." All around the sanctuary hang banners showing the fruit of the Spirit. Evangelism is our way of worship and our train of thought. I preach evangelistically from the pulpit. During a worship service we might read a letter or hear a testimony from someone touched by our outreach. Our radio program "New Life" continually keeps the message of evangelism before the people. All of this keeps our momentum going and keeps our people aware that the greatest job of the Christian life is seeing other souls come to Christ.

We try to emphasize that we are all part of evangelism. Even though some may be the feet of specific, visible ministries and others are called to support them in prayer, no one feels left out or that he's doing a less important part than anyone else

Charles: What is your evangelistic strategy?

Pastor Davila: After participating in several evangelism clinics, I felt a burden that the church should go beyond its four walls. We have carried that burden since the beginning. I came here as a part-time pastor, a stand-in until the congregation could find someone else. At my very first business meeting with these people, I was scared because I didn't feel called to be a pastor. But I remember thinking then that if I were going to be a part-time pastor the others would have to carry the ministry, too. We are going to go beyond our four walls together. And we did.

We opened a mission about 140 miles away and started the radio ministry. More recently we have focused on the church's responsibilities to this community. We have a weekly jail ministry and every Sunday we go to the Martin Juvenile Correction Center. Martin is the only youth correctional center for all races in Corpus

Christi and we're there every Sunday. Several couples share the Word at nursing homes every Sunday afternoon. We trained all these jail and nursing home ministers in evangelism. That's why they go. We're on a 50,000-watt radio station for an hour and a half on Saturday, and on Sunday we have a thirty-minute radio program. Our family is musically talented, and every so often we schedule a service out of Corpus Christi. Six or eight people will go with us to help in ministry. The services are strongly evangelistic. These musical services take a lot of time away from pastoring, so other people in our congregation bear some of the responsibility of caring for those who need help when I'm out of town. Because they carry that responsibility, they feel a part of the ministry, even of our musical ministry. Our people help each other in their ministries. Everybody is involved in part of the work.

Charles: So you are pastoring, but not spending a lot of time in terms of social visitation?

Pastor Davila: Anytime we have a free Saturday, we get together with five, six, or eight couples in the church because we are hungry for the social times. We're always out on spiritual, evangelistic work, it seems, so when we do get the chance to socialize, we really enjoy it.

Charles: The church seems to relax in your gifts and let you operate as God has directed. The people aren't demanding social pampering. They seem to see the bigger purpose of the Hispanic church.

Pastor Davila: That's true, but that attitude doesn't come overnight. A congregation's thinking matures in that way over a period of years. We have a special congregation, one that's out there with us. They not only support us as pastor but also support the church with a vision of their own work. They see what I am to do and what they are to do. If someone is in need, I will be there. But we only meet needs that need to be met. We rejoice in these good people who don't want to be pampered but instead want to serve the Lord.

Charles: Do you have a training program in personal evangelism?

Pastor Davila: I train people myself, and we bring evangelism clinics right into our local meeting. Nine or ten people from our congregation, many of them with positions in the church, attend an accredited Christian college here in Corpus Christi. They're training for their ministries, preparing themselves for the work.
work.

Charles: Do you have other types of outreach? You mentioned jails and nursing homes.

Pastor Davila: My parents and four other couples founded this church, but they are no longer serving on boards and committees. They minister by counseling and praying for the sick and visiting in hospitals. The rest of the congregation recognizes their work as a ministry. Then every Friday night for nine or ten months a year, the young people meet, youth in one place and singles in another. On Tuesdays we have home meetings for people who would not like to come to a church. Some people are apprehensive about being in a Protestant sanctuary. The leaders know the home groups are a branch of our Wednesday and Sunday services. The groups study the Bible, share personal testimonies, and help meet each other's needs. It's an evangelistic setting.

Another key outreach is the prayer ministry. Every Friday morning eight to ten women meet in my office or the sanctuary to pray for needs. A group of men meets in another place.

Charles: Is regular visitation part of your outreach?

Pastor Davila: I'll give you my personal view—what works for Iglesia de Dios and Gilbert Davila. Personal visitation is important, but many of our ongoing ministries, especially the radio work, already go into thousands of homes. For me, that takes the place of knocking on doors. The ministries bring people in. If they didn't, I would be out knocking on doors.

Charles: Who are you trying to reach?

Pastor Davila: That's easy to answer. We want to reach the unsaved. I can look back with humor at the beginning of my ministry, when I tried to reach everybody—even saved people and people from other churches. I quickly learned that a church can't be built that way. The Lord calls us to preach the gospel to those without Christ. So we go to the jails and the marketplaces.

Charles: So you're not limiting your outreach to Hispanics?

Pastor Davila: God opened doors for us into the total community, which is 95 percent Hispanic. But when we entered the jails, we found 60 to 70 percent Hispanics and a good percentage of blacks and whites. So we could no longer minister there just in Spanish. We had to use English, too. Before long, we'd realized the importance of ministering bilingually in all of our work.

Charles: How are people attracted to this congregation?

Pastor Davila: The radio ministry is strong and draws people. And our people are trained to invite others, even to pick them up and bring them. Some people come because our location makes us visible. We're right on a corner and when people have a need, they know where we are.

Several years ago, I picked up a small poster in Mexico. In English it reads, "At this place, we love, we believe, and we hope." A spirit of love and humility permeates our worship. There's always a joyful spirit. That spirit carries over into the heart of the worship, preaching, and prayer. Our worship is unique because we have a special time of prayer at the altar. We have an altar call for the unsaved, of course, but before that we'll have prayer to anoint the sick or to pray specifically for other needs. We pray in an orderly manner, but it's a special time when people can lose themselves in the group and talk to God.

Charles: What do you do with new converts? How are they assimilated into the body?

Pastor Davila: I knew you'd ask one question about an area in which I'd have to confess we are weak! We do our best when new ones come. I follow them as pastor, but I am a very busy pastor, and sometimes follow-up means a new convert goes with me to the radio station or to San Benito mission. We'll talk and maybe stop to eat. Then I'll pass the new Christian on to my staff. The staff are well-trained, and they train others. I can't train everybody, so I rely on my leaders. If someone doesn't respond to the leaders, I'll step in and help. But the whole area of follow-up needs more work.

Charles: Who are these leaders?

Pastor Davila: David Canales, who has been with me five or six years; Rick Mansfield, who now pastors a church in Albuquerque, New Mexico; Hector Gonzales, who is now pastoring in Phoeniz, Arizona. That's the trouble with these leaders! We train them and then send them to pastor in other places! We have to keep raising up new leaders. And we have local leaders who help, too.

Charles: One of the most beautiful parts of this ministry is this training and sending of young pastors to Spanish-speaking congregations. You are duplicating yourself. That's evidence of a great ministry.

Pastor Davila: It's a scary thing. These young pastors come to me for prayer. They have real fears. Their call is genuine; they know they are called to pastor, and that's why they go. They leave with a humble spirit, knowing that they can't do it alone, but knowing also that the Lord will go with them wherever he calls them to go. In twenty years, we've sent probably nine or ten pastors, four or five of them in the last five years.

Charles: What kind of discipling method do you use?

Pastor Davila: We follow the New Testament method. We encourage Christians to have a good knowledge of the Word of God, to be balanced in their Christian lives and not to waver. We especially stress this if they are going to be leaders. Then they will get all the training possible. Sometimes we'll help pay for the training. Lately we've been blessed as persons in national leadership positions have come to share in seminars in specific areas in which we need much training.

In recent years, I've been discipling just a few people one on one. I pray that God will give those people extra strength because they can do everything I do. When I'm out of the country, they can handle the ministry because they've been trained to preach, teach, and really do anything that needs to be done.

Charles: You've mentioned the jail ministry, the juvenile ministry, and work at nursing homes and hospitals. Is the church involved in any other specialized outreach?

Pastor Davila: Specifically our church is involved in those four areas. Now if another pastor runs a ministry in the parks, we won't try to start another one, but we will help by sending one of our singing groups or a leader to give a personal testimony. We'll support wherever we can, but the four ministries you mentioned are this church's priorities.

Charles: How do you use your own gifts of music as an outreach?

Pastor Davila: In the beginning of our ministry, music was an attention-getter. People came to hear the music and that was great, but because our other ministries weren't ready, the people didn't stay. Now that situation is improved, and we still use our music but with better results. We've produced an album that is circulating in the Spanish community. Music isn't the basis of our ministry, but it's very effective. Sometimes it's hard to separate the music from the preaching.

We run two radio programs, one of which is an hour and a half of music and testimonies. The other broadcast has a preaching format. In both our radio and music ministries, our purpose is not to entertain. Both ministries demand a lot of time, energy, and resources. If it were up to us, sometimes we wouldn't give what it takes. But the Lord calls us to these ministries, and our purpose is to win souls. Radio and music must not be a matter of "Hey, look at me! I'm on the air" or "on television." The ministries have to come from a special calling and a special purpose.

Charles: Are there reasons other than some of these outreach programs for the success of Iglesia de Dios?

Pastor Davila: The right kind of leaders and prayer. And I believe our message bears on our success. We need to preach unity and power, and that message has to come from the entire church. We are part of the body of Christ, and we are a united church for a divided world.

Charles: I also see dynamic leadership as a reason for the success-faithfulness on the part of the leaders and your own charismatic personality, winsomeness, preaching, and music ministry. We don't want to lift up a personality as you say, but God does use men.

Pastor Davila: Yet people get tired of a personality. There has to be more than personality. The pastor and the people have to be excited by what God is doing. That's what is happening here.

Charles: What lessons can be learned from the ministry of this church? What things are you doing that can be shared with others?

Pastor Davila: We are more sensitive to God's spirit than we've ever been. We see how far we've come because we did this or that, but when we analyze the results, all we can say is that the Lord's spirit was here and we were willing. There's a spirit of humility. The Lord has used us so far, and we just want to continue to be here in his name. We just want to be sensitive to the Spirit's call.

Charles: Could other churches learn from your radio ministry?

Pastor Davila: If someone can do it effectively,

yes. But another means of evangelism could be just as effective. Each church must use the gifts God gives to its people.

The church must use its gifts where the world is. That's why we go to the marketplace. One of my church members, an elderly woman, recently lost her husband. It was a rough time for her. At the marketplace, she met a woman who said she was sorry about the husband's death. Our church member said, "God has given me all the strength I need." She ended up praying for the other woman, right there in the store, about a need in that woman's life. Our church is a loving church. But in a practical sense, as this elderly woman showed, we're an evangelistic church.

Discussion

1. Notice how Pastor Davila finds the church's mission in two scriptures—Isaiah 61 and John 11. What scriptures best describe the mission of your congregation?_____

_____

_____

_____

2. List several things Iglesia de Dios has done to "go beyond its four walls." _____

_____

_____

_____

3. Why does Pastor Davila feel that visitation is not very important to his work?_____

_____

_____

_____

Would the same be true in your congregation?

_____

_____

_____

4. What does Pastor Davila feel is a weak aspect of his ministry? _____

_____

_____

_____

What are some of his special strengths or gifts? _____

_____

_____

_____

5. List your pastor's strengths, as you see them. Then spend some time praying for your pastor. _____

_____

_____

_____

"We sent eighteen people from our congregation to form the nucleus of a new church."

Chapter 11

A Small Church Can Be Spiritual, Too
Pastor Gene Moses

Overview

Five thousand people lived in De Soto, Missouri, in 1952. Twenty years later, the population had risen to five thousand nine hundred. A small town not far from St. Louis, De Soto grew up around the Missouri-Pacific Railroad, and the railroad still is the town's major industry. A shoe factory and several small businesses give the town the rest of its commercial base.

As people moved away from St. Louis to the rural and suburban areas around De Soto, the town experienced some growth. Rising gasoline prices in the 1970s hampered commuting, however, and high interest rates prevented families from buying new homes. Growth in De Soto slowed.

Gene Moses grew up in De Soto, left after high school, and returned in 1972 as pastor of the First Church of God. According to Pastor Moses, the town is "playing catch-up," repairing streets, sewer lines, and water lines, developing housing for senior citizens, cleaning up run-down areas. Hurt by the recession and resultant lay-offs, De Soto nevertheless worked hard to develop its park system and creative arts center. Drug abuse caused some problems in De Soto, but the problem does not overwhelm the community. Pastor Moses credits De Soto with determination and a "young spirit."

The Church of God in De Soto was established in the early 1900s as members of a prayer meeting identified themselves with the theology in *The Gospel Trumpet*. The church was pastored then by Samuel Clemens. The congregation moved to its present location in 1928. The Church of God has built a fine reputation in De Soto as a stable congregation, one interested in its community.

Several First Church families have supported the church through three generations. The congregation is a cross-section of townspeople: Teachers, laborers, professionals, and business people worship and work together. About 75 percent of the De Soto congregation are white; the remainder are black. Some black families see the growth in black attendance at First Church as a slur against the local black church, but leaders in the black community continue to come to First Church.

The facilities serve the First Church congregation well at this point, although the sanctuary already is at capacity. The congregation met not long after Pastor Moses arrived to plan long-term goals and has worked hard to accomplish the first two: building a larger fellowship hall and hiring an associate. A third goal, mothering a congregation in one of the growing areas outside De Soto, will allow First Church to continue at its present location. The congregation does not see why it should move the entire church to larger quarters when neighboring towns have no Church of God. The present morning worship attendance is 165, compared with 125 just ten years ago.

Interview

Charles: What's your leadership style here, Gene?

Pastor Moses: I define my leadership by a strong emphasis on lay people. If a layperson can carry a responsibility, I'll let him do it and find something else for myself. I work with the lay people, and there is an openness between us. They are willing to work and they're creative. It's exciting to be their pastor. I see myself as the equipper and coordinator, challenging them to handle the ministry. When major decisions have to be made, we put them to committees. We discuss the situation, and everyone has input. I don't get my way every time.

Charles: How do you develop a positive climate for evangelism? How do you get people excited about witnessing?

Pastor Moses: First, people have to sense the need for evangelism. Our church doesn't believe that evangelism and Christian living are two separate things; to us, it's all one. Being a good neighbor, being honest in business, helping someone—that's a kind of evangelism, too.

Then, the church enjoys a good reputation in De Soto. We maintain our integrity, and we work closely with other churches on community projects. Since I've returned, I've seen good relationships built among the Roman Catholic and Protestant churches. As far as I'm concerned, that cooperation is part of the Church of God message. We emphasize the things we can do together rather than the things that separate us. Even the lay people work together. It's a fine witness to the community.

Charles: What is the evangelistic strategy of First Church?

Pastor Moses: First of all, self-examination. We have to know what evangelism means to us in light of New Testament teaching. We have to apply the principles of discipleship to the needs in our community. We give to foreign missions, of course, but we can't pat ourselves on the back about missions if we don't take care of needs right down the street. This town is very small and there are many churches. We have to let people know that the Church of God is unique. So our evangelistic thrust is to get to know people first. We reach out by going into homes. We want people to know we care about them as individuals.

We maintain a Living File here and we get

leads from local realtors, schools, Welcome Wagon—anywhere we can learn about new people in town. Through the hospital chaplaincy program, I find people who have no church home. If we make contact with someone through the Living File, we'll send an evangelistic team to visit. We'll also send a team if someone visits our church. We never send a team unless we've made contact beforehand. We even make appointments for the teams so people are not caught off-guard.

Charles: Do you have teams that go into homes for friendly, get-acquainted visitation, different from an evangelism call?

Pastor Moses: That's part of our Living File system. We have a meal on Monday nights and then our people visit in town. Afterward they return to church to report. These visits serve to introduce the church to people in the community. We don't train people for these visits; we just tell them to smile! We do have a committee that chooses the people to visit. Teachers visit those who have been absent, first of all. Then we'll visit new people, shut-ins, or people in the hospitals.

We emphasize that everyone involved in visitation is vital to the program. The people who come every week to cook the meal or baby-sit are as important as those who visit. To me, visitation is the life of the church. If the church isn't visiting, it's dying.

Charles: How do you recruit people to visit?

Pastor Moses: As I said, we encourage all of

the Sunday school teachers to visit their classes. Young Christians are eager to visit, especially if they found Christ when someone visited them. I emphasize visitation from the pulpit and we have a minister of visitation who stimulates people to take part. Sometimes we personally invite someone to go visiting. Most people get involved in visiting and witnessing because they're excited about the church.

Charles: Do you train people for personal evangelism?

Pastor Moses: Yes, we have training classes during the Sunday school hour. Our Committee on Evangelism wants everyone in the church to take the class. Even if a person doesn't want to be part of an evangelistic team, he still needs to be able to talk to someone about becoming a Christian. These evangelistic teams visit on Monday nights, too.

Charles: Approximately how many hours per week would you say are spent in purposeful evangelism?

Pastor Moses: Of course, every worship service is geared toward evangelism. Wednesday nights are planned for evangelism through a graded family program. Twelve to fourteen hours each week, I would guess, if you mean structured evangelistic activities.

Charles: Who is your target in De Soto? Who are your trying to reach?

Pastor Moses: To me, the gospel knows no discrimination. We have a multiracial congregation. We'll take the gospel to anyone who is willing to listen.

Charles: How are people attracted to this congregation?

Pastor Moses: As I mentioned before, our reputation draws people. We keep our facilities attractive and our involvement in community affairs makes us visible. The community likes what it sees in our people. There is no atmosphere of judgment here.

Then some people are attracted to me as the hometown preacher. I'm active in Rotary Club, on the Park Board, in Little League football—people see me around town, not just in church.

First Church is a warm place. Our people love one another and offer that love to newcomers. We believe the Christian life is a good life, a joyous life, but we don't pretend a Christian has no problems. We just offer love. I don't think this is something a church can create artifically, but people do have to work at it. People have to be willing to go out of their way to make new people feel welcome.

Charles: First Church is growing and you're seeing new converts. How are new Christians incorporated into this body?

Pastor Moses: First, we recognize them as individuals with particular strengths and weaknesses. We identify the parts of their lives that need nurturing. We have a new convert's class in which we survey their talents to find where they can start working. Some people feel they have nothing to offer the body at first. We see that as a lack of confidence and take extra care to make them feel needed.

Charles: Is the church involved in any specialized ministries? Describe the Contact Program you're involved with.

Pastor Moses: Contact is a twenty-four-hour telephone hot-line. People can call anytime and get help with food, counseling, money for utilities, overnight lodging, and other crisis needs. We try to bridge the gap until long-term help can step in. The Ministerial Alliance started the hot-line, but lay people gradually are taking over. Most of the churches in town take part. As the ministers talked, we realized that we were duplicating efforts to help people with emergency needs. Now we pool our resources through Christ.

Besides Contact, our church ministers in nursing homes.

Charles: Other than effective programming, Gene, why is First Church successful? Is it your preaching? Your Bible emphasis?

Pastor Moses: I guess every pastor would like to consider himself a dynamic preacher. But I consider myself a pastor, not a dynamic preacher. I have to be honest; I don't spend thirty hours on sermons. By communicating with my people and with the Lord in prayer, and by being sensitive to the Holy Spirit, I try to detect the congregation's needs. I believe that Christ had power *with* people, not *over* them. He always drew out the inner resources of the people he met. I have tried to find our strong points as a congregation.

The Bible is our guideline, of course. But we don't dwell on the do nots. We emphasize the Bible's positive force in the Christian life.

Charles: What concepts have you used here that another church might use? What ideas might transfer?

Pastor Moses: First, I have found that the spirituality of a congregation does not depend on its size. And yet, neither does growth mean a church is unspiritual. Growth is exciting. Sometimes a church can manufacture growth with a program, and programs are important if they meet needs. But our congregation won't buy a program just for the sake of doing something new.

Second, I think people come to First Church because they find love and acceptance here. We don't judge them, but we try to lift them to higher levels through God's grace and power. No one pretends to have a corner on understanding.

Then, I think a pastor should listen more to lay people. I have developed mutual respect with our lay people. I listen to them.

Charles: How would you classify First Church? What is your mission in De Soto?

Pastor Moses: Our mission is to reach people who do not know Christ and to nurture the people who do. If we visit and evangelize but forget to nurture, we're just running a treadmill. People drift out the back door. The Christian life has to be a growing, challenging experience.

We're ready to reach anyone who's not already being reached. In the spring of 1983 we started a new congregation in Festus, a town thirteen miles northeast of here. The state's Kingdom Builders office loaned the money to buy the church property and a home for the pastor. Ken Vanderlaan worshiped with us for eight months as he prepared to start this new work, and we sent eighteen more people from our congregation to form the nucleus of the Festus church. By summer, more than forty people were worshiping there.

So we want to reach the lost for Jesus, wherever they are. And we're willing to do whatever it takes to reach them.

Discussion

1. Read Luke 14:12-24, which tells about inviting people to church. Jesus begins by describing a feast; then a disciple points out that the kingdom of God is the greatest feast of all (v. 15), and Jesus drives the point home. What sort of people does Jesus tell us to invite? _____

_____

_____

_____

Will most people accept our invitation or reject it? _____

_____

_____

_____

What should we do when people reject it?____

_____

_____

_____

2. Does your church have a systematic method for inviting people to church, such as the Living File? If not, how might you start such a program?____

_____

_____

_____

3. Explain the difference between the two types of visitation teams at De Soto—the evangelistic teams and the Living File teams. ____

_____

_____

_____

4. Life-style evangelism is not something you "go and do," but rather it is something you "do as you go"—not just in visitation for the church on Monday night, but in the normal flow of your daily communication and interaction with people. How does Pastor Moses do that? ____

_____

_____

_____

5. De Soto's Contact phone ministry helps people with emergency needs. How does your church deal with emergency needs, such as people who need money for food or utilities? women who are beaten by their husbands? lonely people who are trying to commit suicide?‗‗‗‗‗‗

‗‗‗‗‗‗‗‗‗‗‗‗‗‗‗‗‗‗‗‗‗‗‗‗‗‗‗‗‗‗‗‗‗‗‗‗‗‗

‗‗‗‗‗‗‗‗‗‗‗‗‗‗‗‗‗‗‗‗‗‗‗‗‗‗‗‗‗‗‗‗‗‗‗‗‗‗

Chapter 12

"We have four youth programs and a Saturday Club that gives hot meals, recreation, and Bible study to 200 black and Hispanic children each week."

Chapter 12
Grafting New Christians Into the Vine
Pastor Benjamin Reid

Overview

Located on the west side of Los Angeles, First Church of God serves a community composed primarily of middle- to upper-middle-class blacks. One-quarter million people surround First Church, which sits on the edge of the wealthiest black inner-community in Los Angeles. The people who live around First Church are predominantly young adults in single-family homes or apartments.

For all its population and comfortable economic status, the area around First Church is underchurched; that is, the community does not have many significant churches to meet the needs of the people. As more and more families move to the west side from other parts of Los Angeles, Pastor Benjamin Reid sees the need for a viable, strong, worshiping church.

He also sees a crying need for youth activities, since the community lacks even parks or play space. Alert to the needs of youth, First Church opened its Christian school because the area schools are, in Pastor Reid's words, "quite poor."

Finally, Pastor Reid cites the need for counseling in the community: family counseling, crisis counseling, and marital counseling to combat the high divorce rate. In this area many unmarried couples live together, so Pastor Reid believes the church should present a strong family-life emphasis.

First Church reflects its community. About 80 percent of its congregation is under forty years of age. Two-thirds are middle- or lower-middle-class blacks. About half of the congregation have some college education and one-fourth hold graduate degrees. Professional, semiprofessional, middle-range executives, and skilled workers make up a large part of the congregation.

First Church of God has had phenomenal growth, from an average morning attendance of about three hundred in 1974 to fifteen hundred today. A few years ago, they purchased a 4½ acre campus for $825,000 to handle their growing needs. Since purchasing this campus, attendance in the Christian school has escalated from less than 200 to over 400 students and membership in the congregation has risen from 800 in

1979 to over 1500 each Sunday today.

The church raised over $300,000 to remodel a classroom building into a 1,000-seat sanctuary. They have extensively remodeled the remaining four buildings, added a 250-car parking lot and erected a new 2,400 square foot portable classroom building to accommodate growth in church and school activities. The church-school budget exceeds $850,000.

While this internal growth has gone on, the church has sent out six pastors and shared over 100 members with mission churches and new congregations in California. It is the headquarters church of fifty Church of God congregations in Nigeria, Africa and sends monthly support to these churches.

Interview

Charles: Pastor Reid, I sense a positive climate for evangelism in this church. How is that atmosphere generated?

Pastor Reid: First of all, through a strong worship experience. This is a worshiping church and we emphasize a strong pulpit ministry. Second, this church cares. We reach out constantly to meet areas of need in our community. Third, as more people are won through person-to-person evangelism, they in turn have a strong desire to win others. We encourage and channel this desire.

Charles: Do you have an evangelistic strategy?

Pastor Reid: Yes! Our church facility, staff,

members, and every department compose a mighty evangelism factory. We stress that everything we do is pointed to winning and nurturing souls. If it does not fit this purpose, we drop it. In addition, the pastor and three staff persons and the Evangelism Task Force keep evangelism before the church. Third, we have a large number of people committed to various forms of personal soul-winning: (1) door to door, (2) neighborhood Bible study groups, (3) passing out handbills and tracts in shopping centers, and (4) hospital and convalescent home ministry. So both professional staff and lay people have an inner desire, a passion, and a systematic method to reach out and get people saved. Finally, we plan, budget, and program—we utilize our time and money—to carry out the work of evangelism in our community. Fully 12 percent of our total budget is spent in some form of evangelism.

Charles: Do you regularly train your people for evangelism?

Pastor Reid: We have a Lay Institute for Evangelism—the L.I.F.E. program—four times a year. The Art of Personal Soul Winning is a regular class in our ten-week School of Christian Living. Another weekly class in soul winning is taught by two dedicated laypersons.

Charles: How many hours do the people spend in purposeful evangelism within your whole ministry?

Pastor Reid: If you mean planned church evangelistic activities, actual time on the church calendar, 300 to 500 persons each week give at least one hour of their time directly to evangelistic endeavors. By this we mean tract distribution, door-to-door work, convalescent and hospital ministry, youth outreach, senior citizens activity, and drug programs.

Charles: What about regular visitation? Is that a priority here?

Pastor Reid: Yes, by both staff and volunteers. Every one of our eleven staff members visits. We have forty deacons who nurture new converts and visiting is part of their responsibility. Twenty-one undershepherds visit both new prospects and those who are discouraged or delinquent in attendance. We have developed male and female "Search and Rescue Teams" who weekly visit new members, absentees, and dropouts. Visitation ranks high on our priority list, both in general planning and in specific responsibilities.

Charles: So you visit regularly and nurture new people. What kind of people are you trying to reach?

Pastor Reid: We are trying to reach the whole community. We especially try to reach families and young adults. We try to reach the down-and-outers who tend to be neglected by other churches. We try to reach whoever needs help. We try to make the church reflect the community. I think it does.

Charles: What other kinds of specialized ministries do you have besides personal evangelism outreach and visitation?

Pastor Reid: We have a vigorous jail ministry because in this community 60 to 70 percent of those who go to jail are black. And we have a police chaplaincy ministry. We have a flourishing senior citizens work. And, of course, we have a radio program three times a week. We do a prodigious amount of advertising—newspapers, radio, television, billboards, bus benches, and ads on the buses themselves. The advertising identifies us to the community. In November we begin weekly television services featuring our pastor and choirs. We have four youth programs, a Saturday Club that gives hot meals, recreation, and Bible study to 200 black and Hispanic children each week, seven choirs, a "Food for the Hungry" program that feeds over 100 poor families each month, a Christian Cinema, Church Athletic League, Boy and Girl Scout Troops, Teen Boys' Club, Drug Counseling Program and Referral Service. We sponsor "School of the Prophets" which provides training for 40 to 60 ministers a year.

Charles: I notice in your advertising that you stress "membership." What do you mean by that term?

Pastor Reid: Contrary to many Church of God congregations, we believe church membership is very important. We have formal church membership here. We assign every member to our New Members Class which is a six-week orientation class. A Church of God doctrine study booklet is given to each member along with a membership manual that outlines the duties and responsibilities of a church member. In our morning services, we invite people not only to salvation, but also to church membership. We believe a person accepts tremendous responsibility to the body of Christ when he becomes a member of that body. He is expected to become a productive, soul-winning, giving, ministering part of the Body. Real church members do not come casually to hear a message and "receive a blessing." They come to grow and serve the Lord.

So we make a lot of this business of church membership. We keep membership statistics and a membership list, and those who drift away in spite of our efforts do not remain on our list. In my opinion, the Church of God tends to be too casual about a person's responsibility to the body of Christ, and I consider that a weakness of our movement. No one is counted as a member who does not make public commitment to this local congregation and authenticate that commitment through faithful involvement in the church and its activities.

Charles: When new converts come in, how do you assimilate them into the church?

Pastor Reid: When someone becomes a part of the fellowship, we immediately give him or her a "big brother" or "big sister"—an established member of the church who makes the convert familiar with the church. Then we urge new members to take part in a Christian Basis and Growth Class, taught by the associate pastor.

New people receive a packet that gives them a bird's-eye view of the Church of God, its teachings, our local organization, our emphasis, our outreach, and our giving patterns. The deacons are responsible to contact new converts and help them find their places in the fellowship. Every new member is personally interviewed by one of our staff pastors who seeks to help the new member locate just where he or she is spiritually, what he or she needs spiritually and the best means of meeting that need. Our undershepherd groups, in which five to seven people meet with the undershepherds in their neighborhood, also help to integrate new people into the work here. Since each new member fills out an interest profile, the church office notifies the auxiliary or department in which the new member expresses interest.

Charles: Besides the specialized ministries and evangelism, why is First Church of God successful? The church obviously is growing. Why?

Pastor Reid: Because we care. People come because of personal contact and word-of-mouth promotion. A survey in March of 1983 showed that 78 percent of our new members over the last ten years have come directly from personal contact with one of our lay people. We make big efforts in advertising, but that doesn't make the difference. Nor do evangelistic crusades and revivals. Most people come and take part in this church because their neighbors, loved ones, friends, or co-workers bring them here.

Then, too, this church has a strong pulpit ministry. We're strong on Bible teaching and many young adults come because of that Bible teaching. Wednesday night prayer meetings are totally devoted to Bible teaching and they're some of the most exciting services we have. We offer a broad range of other activities, too. Whatever the need, we offer something to meet that need. The warm services and presence of the Holy Spirit have attracted many people to First Church. We emphasize the traditional fervor and fire of the Black church tradition. We are a joyful, singing, worshiping church.

Charles: If you had to categorize this church, what would you say? What best describes First Church of God?

Pastor Reid: As I said before, we care. We care about every age group. We care about drug addicts, about families, about youth, about senior citizens, about former convicts, about the poor, about the middle class. We are a caring church.

We believe that our strong evangelistic thrust has to be backed up with personal care for the community's physical, emotional, and mental needs. Our program is oriented to meeting people's needs, not to the survival of the church.

Discussion

1. Several times in the course of this interview, Pastor Reid said that First Church of God stands out as a *caring* church. List some of the ways they show their caring for the community, and list some ways your church shows your community that you care.

2. Read the following scriptures and note how the first-century church cared for people in their community:

Acts 2:44-45,   4:32-35   *How the Church Cared*

Acts 3:1-8   5:14-16

Acts 6:1-7   1 Tim. 5:9-10

3. First Church uses advertising to good effect. They invest a sizable budget in ads for radio, TV, newspaper, billboards, and so forth. What opportunities does your church have to advertise the work you're doing? (Be sure to list opportunities for free advertising.) _____

_____

_____

_____

4. Many Church of God people would disagree with Pastor Reid's view of church membership. The Bible does not say a local church must keep a formal membership roll, but Pastor Reid thinks that is a good idea. He says, "We believe a person accepts tremendous responsibility to the body of Christ when he becomes a member of that body." What do you think? ___

_____

_____

_____

Chapter 13

"Our PILLARS program trains our people for effective ministry."

Chapter 13
Positive Enthusiasm
Pastor Howard Baker

Overview

Walla Walla is a farming community of twenty-five thousand people. The Washington State Penitentiary is located in Walla Walla and the community boasts three small colleges—Whitman, Community, and Advent. The town has no industry and city leaders do not seek to attract any. Unless young people choose to farm, many of them prefer to move to larger cities with more opportunity. Walla Walla has strong Seventh-Day Adventist and Mormon groups, but the State of Washington overall has the lowest percentage of church attendance among the fifty states.

The Walla Walla area struggles with drug and alcohol abuse among its young people. To combat that abuse, First Church of God is planning a family activity center and has just completed a new sanctuary. On the drawing board are a large gym and related support systems for a stronger youth ministry. As it is, the church's youth ministry suffers for lack of space. The worship attendance has grown from two hundred to four hundred and twenty in the past ten years.

The Walla Walla congregation is well-balanced. Farmers, county extension agents, business people, salespeople, truck drivers, accountants, teachers, and hospital staff work side by side in ministry. The church leadership form the church council, which is composed of six representatives at large and the chairperson of each board and committee. A board of trustees takes care of the physical plant and finances.

Interview

Charles: What is your style of leadership, Pastor Baker?

Pastor Baker: I came to Walla Walla in September 1969. I believe in long pastorates. A pastor needs two or three years to get his roots down, get to know people, win their confidence, and analyze their needs. Our staff follow written job descriptions, and each one works with certain of our boards and committees. Ernie LaFont handles shepherding and missions, and Frank LaFont serves as the senior adult minister. Ted Usher is minister of music. Danny Garman directs the youth work. I am not threatened by staff leadership or lay leadership. Having multiple staff means moving over and giving that staff room to lead and letting them take credit, too. We delegate responsibility, training our lay people to minister with confidence. We work to build our lay leadership. For example, a few weeks ago we invited all the trustees to come forward in the service. We joined in prayer and encouraged the congregation to pray for them as well. We recognize our leaders.

To put my leadership style in a phrase, I'd call it positive enthusiasm. I take some kidding—someone will say to me, "Pastor, we are here to see what is new today and enjoy your enthusiasm." I see the church as an orchestra and myself as the conductor who keeps everything flowing smoothly. Everyone can't play the drums or the horn. My job is to motivate people. When the Holy Spirit leads, we produce a beautiful sound.

Charles: How do you help people be enthusiastic about evangelism? What's your strategy?

Pastor Baker: In my time here, we've held only two revivals, and we don't plan to hold any others. Evangelism is a natural life-style. For example, one woman recently led a young mother to the Lord through a women's class. The woman brought this new Christian to me and we prayed together, talked about baptism, and I gave her some study materials. She's meeting weekly with the woman who won her. They study together. That to me is evangelism— a natural, everyday, ongoing way of life, in school, on the job, or in the neighborhood. It's a family operation. It's sharing the faith constantly, not just making a weak effort here and there.

Charles: How do you make that natural evangelism happen?

Pastor Baker: Through teaching, preaching, personal contact, and encouragement. Our PILLARS program trains our lay people for effective ministry. PILLARS mean *P*eople *I*n *L*eadership *L*earning, *A*chieving, *R*eaching, *S*erving, and is based on Ephesians 4. We run three seven-week sessions each year.

Charles: How many hours a week do you spend on purposeful evangelism?

Pastor Baker: Sixty-five to seventy hours. To me it's all purposeful evangelism. Trying to reach the lost, to find an exciting life-style through Jesus Christ—that's all we do.

Charles: What specialized ministries of outreach do you include in your ministry?

Pastor Baker: We're involved in Soul and Support, a rescue mission. Every third Sunday we preach at the Odd Fellows Home services.

We have home Bible studies that involve the whole neighborhood. And we have the radio ministry. We don't work in the penitentiary; unless people are specially trained, that ministry is too much for them. We have the largest Men's Fellowship this side of the Mississippi River. The men cook their breakfast, invite special speakers, encourage one another. It builds the men. And on Sundays, we are thrilled to see husbands with their wives, not just women alone.

We emphasize missions, too. In the last five years we've given $105,000, a commendable sum for a little farming community. Our church responds to the missions challenge.

From that we move to seven different categories: Lay Ministries of Evangelism, Lay Ministers of Christian Education, and the Bethel Program, which is the backbone of the training. A lay person receives forty-two hours of credit for the Bethel Program. We offer other courses, ninety-eight in all. Once a lay person is graduated from these courses, he receives recognition as an actual lay minister of this church.

My evangelistic strategy begins with not being afraid of the altar. We serve communion at the altar, giving people an opportunity to kneel there. We believe in the altar, and we invite people to come in every service, but we don't pressure anyone into coming.

Our music program reaches out for us. We broadcast our 11:00 A.M. service each Sunday live on radio and we have a Dial-a-Message telephone ministry. We don't rely on advertising because people get used to it and pass over it. But our best strategy happens when our lay people invite their neighbors. (With our shepherding program, we have in essence twenty-five lay pastors on the firing line. Those lay pastors are the nervous system of the church.)

Charles: Do you have regular training for evangelism?

Pastor Baker: As part of the PILLARS program. And I've trained some people to use the

Four Spiritual Laws. We not only have a missions program; our whole church is on mission. Whether the task is a pancake breakfast or a women's missionary group, the focus is on missions.

Charles: Explain the shepherding program you mentioned.

Pastor Baker: About twenty-five families are shepherds. Sometimes ten to fifteen families will visit the church on a Sunday, and our shepherds will visit each one before the week is over. A staff person visits them, too, so each visitor hears from a lay person and a pastor. We leave a Visitor's Welcome Packet which describes our church and our program. And if, for example, the family has children who would be interested in our Explorers program, we'll send an Explorers teacher to visit them, too.

Here's how we got started. After studying a Garden Grove Community Church idea, we pinpointed every one of our families on a map. Each pin had a little name tag. Then we put a fence around every six or seven families and finished with fourteen zones. We trained the shepherding families for seven weeks and turned them loose. They said, "How do I do this? How do you want me to do that?" I said, "Do it the way you want to. Use your personality. Be comfortable with it." We urge the shepherds to become involved with their families. For instance, one shepherd met a family who'd been coming to church just a few weeks before they went on vacation. The shepherd mowed and watered their lawn while they were gone.

Every Monday, the names of families missing from church the day before are entered in a book according to zone. The secretary sends each shepherd a letter, and by Tuesday evening every shepherd knows whom he needs to visit or call. Visitors are listed, too, and I expect the shepherd to call on them. Even if a family just took their boat to the lake for the weekend, the shepherd visits them. People like to know they were missed.

A shepherd is someone who cares for people. Our twenty-five shepherds are out on the cutting edge. They let us know what really is happening out there.

Charles: What kind of people are you trying to reach here at First Church?

Pastor Baker: We try to reach them all. We have a couple from Nigeria, Africa. We have Hispanics who came here several years ago following the crops. They bought a home and stayed. Every soul is valuable, and we run the gamut.

Charles: Why do people come to this church? What attracts them?

Pastor Baker: People who come here get excited and tell other people. I hear it every week: "There's a spirit about that church." "They are so friendly and they make you feel wanted." We try to make every service as beautiful and inspiring as we possibly can so that people will be glad they came to church. I try to make the message uplifting. And it's important to have a program for every member of the family, to give each one an opportunity to grow.

The church is open to the community. For example, the 4-H uses our facilities for their awards banquet every year. We believe in encouraging people to beat a path to our door. The facilities should be used more than just on Sunday.

Charles: When a person becomes a Christian, how do you incorporate him into the life of the church?

Pastor Baker: I encourage many new Christians to get involved in the Bethel Program, which overviews the whole Bible. We try to get them involved. As they're involved, we see spiritual growth. We involve new converts in Bible Explorers, a Tuesday night program for children. The children memorize and recite books of the Bible. The new Christians help with the class and they hear the Scriptures over and over—there's double method in our madness! We try to get acquainted with people and then direct them to others who can look after them and help them grow. We take them through a pastor's class, but they really need contact with other lay people in a small group atmosphere. So we steer new converts into home Bible studies and prayer groups.

Charles: Where do these conversions happen?

Pastor Baker: Evangelism happens everywhere. People come to my office or my home. I go to their homes. One man met me in the parking lot as we were striping it. He said he wanted to talk, so we went to my office and I led him to the Lord. We see more conversions on a one-to-one basis than in public meetings. We saw nine conversions one Sunday in Children's Church. Our co-director of Christian education leads many people to Christ. One man wrote his own tract; he's led more than a thousand people to Jesus. People come here to church and we train them, disciple them, so they have the tools to share their faith.

We constantly stress that God has saved them for a reason—to help someone else. We tell them to witness to their own experience; no one can argue with a personal experience. Christ working in their lives gives them authority.

Charles: How do you develop your lay leaders? How do you get them involved in leadership?

Pastor Baker: One of the turning points for our church came several years ago when we developed our leaders' retreats. We pulled in thirty-five to forty key leaders and assigned five to a car. The driver was responsible to keep the conversation going. The group could talk about anything concerning church, pro or con, and someone in the car took notes. This same group stayed together throughout the retreat. At the retreat site, we started by enthusiastically sharing some exciting things that were happening at church. We showed the film *It Couldn't Be Done*. Then we sent the groups off again to brainstorm more ideas, more things they wanted the church to accomplish. Midway through the twenty-four-hour retreat, the groups had listed eighty-four concerns. Then each leader voted on those concerns, giving ten points to the concern deemed most important, nine to the next, and so on. We added their votes and discovered that finding a youth minister headed the list of priorities. The group decided to work on the top ten concerns during that year. We've retreated like that several times. It's an effective way to hear the layperson.

Charles: Who went with you on the retreat?

Pastor Baker: Key leaders. We hand-picked them and included the board of trustees, Christian education directors, departmental supervisors—those who make up the church council.

Charles: You used the term *turning point?*

Pastor Baker: Things were moving before then, but that first retreat pushed us forward. We sow seeds at those retreats and they later blossom into fruit. Sometimes we present an idea, and the council isn't ready for it, or our presentation is premature. But the seed is planted and when the time is right, the leaders pick up that idea and go with it. That happened with the PILLARS program. I presented it and council voted it down. Two years later, they unanimously voted it in. The church was ready for it.

Discussion

1. Pastor Baker describes his leadership style as "positive enthusiasm." In the interviews we've read, which other pastors had this quality? _____

_____

_____

Describe *enthusiasm*.

_____

_____

_____

2. Pastor Baker says they don't plan to hold any more revival meetings because "evangelism is a natural life-style." How do revival meetings promote evangelism? _____

_____

_____

Why aren't revival meetings as well attended as they were years ago? _____

_____

_____

3. Pastor Baker highlights the value of setting good habits in people's lives—the habit of meeting in the church building, the habit of kneeling at the altar, and so forth. Read what the Bible says in Ephesians 4:17-24 about habits. According to this scripture, how are ungodly habits formed? _____

_____

_____

_____

According to this Scripture, how are godly habits formed?_____

_____

_____

_____

What could your church do to help people form godly habits?_____

_____

_____

_____

4. Walla Walla has a strong men's program—in fact, the largest men's fellowship in the Western states. What seems to attract men to their fellowship?_____

_____

_____

_____

5. Walla Walla leans upon the work of its twenty-five shepherds. List some of the things these shepherds do: _____

_____

_____

_____

Review the work of a *deacon* in the New Testament church (Acts 6:1-7; 1 Tim. 3:8-10). How do the shepherds fulfill some functions of *deacons?*_____

_____

_____

_____

How might shepherds aid the ministry of your church? _____

_____

_____

_____

Chapter 14

Common Characteristics in Growing Churches

These thirteen churches—from Akron, Ohio, to Walla Walla, Washington—are success stories within the Church of God. This is a positive and joyful time for these congregations and others like them. Some churches stagnate with a maintenance ministry, but these churches are bursting at the seams. They are growing and maturing. Lost people are finding Christ. Needs are being met. What are the secrets of this kind of evangelistic growth?

Location apparently is not one of the secrets. Third Street Church in Washington, D.C. thrives in an inner-city neighborhood while Salem Church in Dayton, Ohio, flourishes on that city's outskirts.

Could *history* be a factor? How, then, can

three-year-old Riverchase South Church in Birmingham be compared with eighty-year-old First Church in De Soto, Missouri?

Do *economics* play a part? The church in Newport, Tennessee, serves an Appalachian area with success equal to that of the Clairemont Church in suburban San Diego, California.

What, then, is the secret?

There is no one answer. But vital to each of these thirteen churches is a commitment to an evangelistic life-style. These churches asked hard questions: "What are we supposed to be doing? What is the reason for our existence as a local congregation?" And they found biblical answers. They defined their purpose as evangelism and provided strategies to fulfill that purpose. While these churches serve areas that differ economically, racially, and even culturally, they follow a few common principles.

Deep Committed Love

These growing congregations share a compassionate spirit that moves them to give themselves away for Christ's sake. While they minister inside the walls of their church, they focus on people outside the walls as well. Their programs draw outsiders in; insiders go out through planned efforts to reach the lost. Behind this outward focus these churches have an obviously deepening love and commitment to Jesus Christ and to the work of the body of Christ in their community. Each church says, "We are here to win this city to Jesus Christ." This is not a flippant statement but a passion. Pastors believe it, preach it, and demonstrate it by their life-style.

They have a burden for souls like the burden of John Welch. This Irish preacher used to pray seven to eight hours every day. He kept a plaid blanket on his bed in which he wrapped himself when he felt he must rise during the night to pray. His wife once found him lying face down on the ground outside, wrapped in the plaid blanket and weeping. She complained that he would catch cold. Welch replied, "O woman, I have the souls of three thousand to answer for, and I know not how it is with many of them."[1]

Identification with the Community

These congregations take their neighbors seriously. In most cases, they have surveyed their communities, testing and evaluating needs and then striving to meet those needs. Some have stumbled upon a need quite unexpectedly and then planned a strategy to minister to that need. One pastor said, "If you meet the needs of the community, it will beat a path to your door. If you want the unchurched to visit the church, you must discover what will bring them to you." In each of these thirteen cases, people of the community know the church cares about their spiritual and physical needs.

Dr. David Schwartz of Detroit tells of stopping at a gas station in Cincinnati late one afternoon and noticing a lot of cars at the pumps. In a moment, he realized why. The attendant filled the tank, checked under the hood, and cleaned the windshield. He then walked up to Dr. Schwartz and said, "Pardon me, sir. It's been a dusty day. Let me clean the inside of your windshield."

The attendant quickly did so. Dr. Schwartz was impressed. The cleaning improved his night vision considerably. In the next three months, he made eight more trips through Cincinnati and stopped at this station each time. Each time he stopped, they had plenty of business—even at 4 A.M.[2]

Growing churches have learned this principle, too. They've made a habit of serving people.

Commitment to the Word

Within these churches, the Bible stands paramount. From the pastor's sermons, through Sunday school, to small Bible study groups, emphasis on the Word is strong. New converts are encouraged in every possible way to anchor their faith through study of the Bible.

Evelyn Christiansen is a noted leader of women's Bible studies. She often gives the group a passage of Scripture, tells them to disperse, and then calls them back to hear what the Holy Spirit revealed to each woman just by reading the Word. She relates what happened at a weekend retreat when she did this:

I asked my usual "Did God say anything to you?" question, and one member said, "Yes, he did."

"What did he say?"

"He said that I didn't know the Scriptures. Well, that's why I'm here—because my church doesn't teach the Bible, and I want to learn the Scriptures. But God also said, 'You don't know the power of God either!' " [cf. Mark 12:24]

"Would you like to know the power of God?"

"Yes, I would."

"Right now?" After all, we hadn't even *started* the lesson yet, and it certainly wasn't time for application.

"Yes, right now." And before I even started to teach, she bowed her head and accepted Jesus as her Savior.[3]

Growing churches have learned that people get saved through reading the Word. So they emphasize Bible study.

Leadership with Vision

Leadership is a vital key. Some leaders are strong-minded and aggressive, but other kinds of leadership are just as effective. One lay person said of the pastor, "He's not a strong preacher or even a strong leader, but he's in love with Jesus and he has taught us to love Jesus, too."

Effective leadership enthusiastically believes in what the church is doing. The leaders of these thirteen congregations have a vision and are committed to see that vision become reality. The leaders are committed to giving significant parts of their lives to developing evangelistic life-style congregations. The pastors plan to invest in long pastorates; short-term pastorates do not produce long-lasting results. The staff members take time to build a level of trust among lay leaders. They wait patiently for growth, knowing that growth is a *by-product* of effective ministry, not an objective.

Redefined Lay Leadership

In each of these churches, laymen and laywomen are training and equipping for ministry. They visit, witness, teach, and administrate. In fact, lay people have come out of the pews to fill full-time staff positions in four of these churches. Laypersons have redefined their roles as Christians in all of these churches: they are ministers, obligated to discover their gifts and then use them.

Commitment to Balance

These thirteen congregations strive for balance among instruction, fellowship, witness, and worship. They do not build on gimmicks. They build on *strategies* designed to reach their clearly stated purpose. Worship fosters a spontaneous joy. Altars are open and attractive. Singing delights and warms the heart. Evangelistic preaching calls people to salvation in worship services, not just in local home visitation.

Courage to Dream

The churches interviewed share a willingness to dream, to take risks, to venture in the name of Jesus. They consistently reach out with assurance, even though resources may not be readily available to finalize their dreams.

Ruby Kitchen felt the Church of God should start a children's home, and she talked with several ministers about it. She felt that if a fiery minister would head up the work, people would get behind him and the home would be established. But no one agreed to take charge of the project. Finally, her father-in-law, Moses Kitchen said, "Ruby, until someone with a real burden spearheads this job, it will never be done. You obey God, and He will make a way." So Ruby set out to organize Hope Hill Children's Home.[4]

Growing churches have learned what Ruby learned: when you obey God, he will make a way.

Commitment to Prayer

Finally, these growing evangelisic life-style congregations anticipate vitality and growth. They prepare for it. They have entered into the ministry of prayer. Prayer involves us in the mission of God. Praying for a growing, evangelistic congregation is bound to influence the direction and fruit of the congregation. The chronic illness of a stagnated church is lethargy, and the symptom of lethargy is prayerlessness. The great evangelist Henry Martyn once wrote in his diary:

Devoted too much time and attention to outward public duties of the ministry. But this was a mistaken conduct, for I have learned that neglect of much and fervent communion with God in meditation and prayer is not the way to redeem the time nor fit me for public ministry.

I rightly attribute my present deadness

to want of sufficient time and tranquility for private devotion. Want of more reading, retirement and private devotion, I have little mastery over my own tempers. An unhappy day for me for want of more solitude and prayer. If there be anything I do, if there be anything I leave undone, let me be perfect in prayer.[5]

Perhaps these principles for growing an evangelistic life-style congregation seem too simple to be effective. They are simple, but real. Churches based on these principles are growing. I hope you will find some of the principles and strategies helpful. Very likely, they will stimulate you to develop methods suited to your own congregation in your own community.

Growing Pains

For any congregation with an evangelistic life-style, evangelism never ends. There are no shortcuts to winning your community for Christ. You will not find precise, patent formulas. Each local church fills a unique role. Each community is unique. What succeeds in one area may fail in another. What appeals to one congregation may puzzle another. That is the challenge: to seek innovative ways to reach people for Christ.

A congregation should ask itself whether its programs carry out the witness it claims to believe. Do the programs impede and choke the witness of the congregation? Is the congregation involved only in maintenance ministry, in safeguarding the status quo? If so, you may need to dismantle some structures and programs. Existing programs indicate what your congregation believes to be important. So examine your church's structure and emphasis.

Before you decide to carry on business as usual in the local church, remember two important guidelines:

1. Programs and methods are *not* sacred.
2. Principles *are* sacred. They transcend programs and geographical locations.

A congregation's programs must propel the church into evangelism ministry, not insulate it from ministry. The evangelistic effectiveness of a congregation stands fundamentally on your genuineness as the community of God. Aside from these general guidelines, be alert to other growing pains as your congregation seeks evangelism as a life-style.

Not an Elite Work

People who are not involved in evaluating the church's ministry may feel left out. They may think a Monday night evangelism class is an elite group. Be sure to inform all church people of evangelism opportunities. Encourage them to be involved in all levels of outreach and ministry.

Whose Responsibility

Every Christian should understand that lifestyle evangelism is his or her responsibility. Regardless of how much training he or she has received, each should be a witness for the Lord. Believers not involved in an organized outreach effort are tempted to say, "Witnessing is someone else's responsibility."

Evangelism Never Ends

Evangelism must be the constant thrust of the church. It is not a hit-or-miss proposition. It is the ongoing concern of every Christian. After a church emphasizes evangelism, some congregations have an initial surge of commitment—followed by a cooling of that commitment. Evangelism should be a constantly high priority for your congregation.

Evangelism Is Not Superficial

Finally, persons who are not aware of the outreach and witness of the church may attribute growth to superficial success factors. They will be like the man who saw several people make decisions for Christ during a worship service. He remarked to the pastor, "You sure preached a good sermon today, preacher." As if the sermon alone were responsible for the conversions! The man did not know that several of the new converts had been visited, loved, and brought to their decision by consistent lay witnesses. Certainly, the sermon helped draw the new converts to Jesus Christ. But any pastor knows that without prior cultivation and prayer by lay people, there is little to harvest on Sunday morning.

Notes

1. E. M. Bounds, *Purpose in Prayer* (Chicago: Moody Press, n.d.), 56.

2. David J. Schwartz, *The Magic of Thinking Big* (Hollywood, Calif.: Wilshire Book Co., 1959), 136.

3. Evelyn Christensen, *Two by Evelyn ("Lord, Change Me!")* (Wheaton, Ill.: SP Publications, 1979), 186.

4. Ruby Martin Kitchen, *The Valleys and Hills of Hope* (Nashville: Impact Books, 1969), 77.

5. Henry Martyn, quoted by E. M. Bounds, *Purpose in Prayer* (Chicago: Moody Press, n.d.), 61-62.

Chapter 15

How Are You Doing?

You've just read interviews with the pastors of thirteen growing, dynamic churches. All of them have made evangelism a way of life. As Pastor John Boedeker said, to them witnessing is "as natural as breathing."

How about your congregation? How well are you developing a life-style of evangelism?

The following questionnaire may help you find out. It's not an infallible test, of course. But you'll find that it's a fairly reliable gauge of how faithful your church has been to Jesus' Great Commission to "go into all the world."

Mission

1. Describe in one sentence your church's mission. What is your purpose for being here?

_____

_____

2. How many of your people agree on this mission?

_____ Most _____ Many _____ Few

3. How is your community any different because your church is there? (You might find it easier to answer the opposite: How would your community be different if your church were *not* there?)

Programs

1. List the programs that help you fulfill the mission of your church. _____

_____

_____

_____

2. List the programs that *don't* help you fulfill the mission of your church. (Put an *X* beside those that should be eliminated.) _____

_____

_____

_____

3. Now divide these programs into categories—"In-reach" (programs that help people already in the church) and "out-reach" (programs that help people outside the church). Notice which type of program predominates in your church:

4. What programs train people to serve in the church?_____

_____

_____

_____

5. What programs train people to serve in the community? _____

_____

_____

_____

Experience

1. Check the word in each pair that best describes the worship services of your church:

_____ Joyful	or	_____ Solemn
_____ Thoughtful	or	_____ Emotional
_____ Loud	or	_____ Quiet
_____ Warm	or	_____ Cool
_____ Structured	or	_____ Spontaneous

2. How many of your people are involved in home Bible study groups?
____ Most ____ Many ____ Few ____ None

3. How many of your people are involved in prayer support groups?
____ Most ____ Many ____ Few ____ None

4. How many of your people are taking training to learn how to lead someone to Christ?

_____ Most _____ Many _____ Few _____ None

5. How would you rate the quality of your spiritual life?

_____ Excellent _____ Good _____ Fair _____ Poor

6. What ideas have you gained from these interviews that might help your church improve the quality of your spiritual life? _____

_____

_____

_____

Vision

1. Write a brief description of your church ten years from now. (Describe the worship services, the type of people attending, the programs being sponsored, the size of the congregation, the facility, the community, and so forth.) _____

_____

_____

_____

2. What single Scripture passage best describes the direction you feel your church should take for the future? _____

_____

_____

_____

3. What aspects of your church's life excite you the most and give you hope for the future?

_____

_____

_____

Goals (examples)

1. Our goal is to make _____ visits each week beginning on _____ (date).

2. Our goal is to locate and cultivate _____ unsaved prospects by _____ (date).

3. Our goal is to enlist prayer partners by _____ to pray for the unsaved.

4. Our goal is to conduct _____ evangelistic events, such as revivals, renewal services, or preaching mission weekends by _____.

5. Our goal is to train and equip _____ church members to become effective witnesses for Jesus Christ by _____.

6. Our goal is to train _____ persons to encourage and help new converts in their walk with Christ.

Resources/Bibliography

EFFECTIVE WITNESS HELP Evangelism Clinic

HELP, an acronym for *H*ow-to *E*vangelism *L*eadership *P*rogram, is the name of the personal evangelism training offered by the Board of Church Extension and Home Missions, P. O. Box 2069, Anderson, Indiana 46018. The clinic is designed to train persons to witness in the normal daily pattern of life. Continued intensive training in the local church (twelve weeks) is urged at the close of the clinic.

Evangelism Explosion

The aim of this training is to help churches, pastors, and laity to learn better how to do person-to-person evangelism and how to train others to do the same. The emphasis is on simply learning to tell the gospel in a positive and gracious manner. (*Evangelism Explosion,* Tyndale House Publishers, 336 Gunderson Drive, Wheaton, Illinois 60687.)

Tell Witness Skill Training

Tell Witness Skill Training is a new approach to personal evangelism training. Incorporating the TELL set projector, the system will stimulate, equip, and involve persons in personal witnessing to the point that witnessing becomes a life-style. Through filmstrips and personal study or group interaction, persons learn a growth process that continues to develop long after the ten-week series is completed. (Tell Witness, P. O. Box 2069, Anderson, Indiana 46018.)

L.I.F.E. Weekend

L.I.F.E. is a weekend experience in renewal during which time a coordinator and a group of laypersons from other congregations and communities come to a local church to share their faith, lead small groups, and share in worship services. For information contact the following: Dale Warman c/o First Church of God, 3300 NE 78 St., Vancouver, Washington 98665 or Central Community Church of God, 1201 S. Market Street, Wichita, Kansas 67211.